Liv B's
Vegan on a Budget

Liv B's
Vegan ON A Budget

**112 Inspired & Effortless
Plant-Based Recipes**

Olivia Biermann

Robert
ROSE

Library and Archives Canada Cataloguing in Publication

Biermann, Olivia, 1994–, author

Liv B's vegan on a budget: 112 inspired and effortless plant-based recipes / Olivia
Biermann.

Includes index.

ISBN 978-0-7788-0625-7 (softcover)
1. Vegan cooking. 2. Low budget cooking. 3. Cookbooks.
I. Title. II. Title: Vegan on a budget.

TX837.B53 2019   641.5'636   C2018-906358-0

Disclaimer

The recipes in this book have been carefully tested by our kitchen and our tasters. To the
best of our knowledge, they are safe and nutritious for ordinary use and users. For those
people with food or other allergies, or who have special food requirements or health issues,
please read the suggested contents of each recipe carefully and determine whether or not
they may create a problem for you. All recipes are used at the risk of the consumer.

We cannot be responsible for any hazards, loss or damage that may occur as a result of
any recipe use.

For those with special needs, allergies, requirements or health problems, in the event of
any doubt, please contact your medical adviser prior to the use of any recipe.

Cover and book design: Margaux Keres
Cover and interior photography: Brilynn Ferguson
Editor: Meredith Dees
Copyeditor, Proofreader & Indexer: Gillian Watts
Recipe Editor: Jennifer MacKenzie
Food Styling: Dara Sutin
Prop Styling: Rayna Schwartz

The publisher gratefully acknowledges the financial support of our publishing program
by the Government of Canada through the Canada Book Fund.

Canada

Published by Robert Rose Inc.
120 Eglinton Avenue East, Suite 800, Toronto, Ontario, Canada M4P 1E2
Tel: (416) 322-6552 Fax: (416) 322-6936
www.robertrose.ca

Printed and bound in Canada

1 2 3 4 5 6 7 8 9 TCP 19 18 17 16 15 14 13 12 11

To my YouTube subscribers and online
family: You changed my life. Thank you for
your support and love every single day.

Table of Contents

INTRODUCTION IX
GETTING STARTED 1

STAPLES & SAUCES 9
Cashew Milk Two Ways 10
Marinara Sauce 12
Veggie Gravy 13
Orange Almond Butter Sauce 14
Creamy Hummus Salad Dressing 15
Thai Peanut Sauce 16
Vegan "Honey Mustard" Dip 17
Spicy Lime Mayo 18
Cheese Sauce 19
Vegan Ricotta Two Ways 20
Best-Ever Tofu Cubes 22
Seitan "Sausage" Crumbles 24
Sliceable Seitan 25
Vanilla Almond Butter 26
Caramel Sauce 27

BREAKFAST & BRUNCH 29
Strawberry Citrus Smoothie 31
Pre-Workout Berry Smoothie 32
Post-Workout Choco Smoothie 32
Tropical Green Smoothie 35
Berry Smoothie Bowls 36
Spiced Coconut Granola 39
Overnight Muesli 40
Empty-Jar Overnight Oats 43
Blueberry Pie Oatmeal 44
Cinnamon Peach Oatmeal 47

Warm Apples and Almond Butter Bowls 48
Almond Butter Toast with
Caramelized Bananas 49
Mini Chocolate Lava Pancakes 51
Half-Baked Cookie Dough Pancakes 52
Crispy Breakfast Potatoes 55
Breakfast Tea Biscuits 56
Crispy Avocado Open-Face Sandwiches 59
Chickpea Scramble 61
Southwest Scramble Toast 63
Savory Breakfast Bowls 64

SNACKS & SMALL BITES 67
Crispy Tofu Dippers 69
Avocado Fried Toast 70
Sweet and Salty Popcorn 73
Cheesy Warm Nachos 74
Maple Cinnamon Pecans 77
Spicy Mango Salsa 78
Five-Minute Guacamole 78
Chocolate Chia Pudding 81
Vegan Snackboard with Easy
Spreadable Cheese 82
Sun-Dried Tomato and
Spinach Pinwheels 85
Chocolate-Dipped Fruit Pops 86
Chocolate Chip Banana Bread in a Mug 89
Snickerdoodle Mug Cake 90

SOUPS & SIDES 93

Famous Lasagna Soup 94

Takeout Thai Curry Coconut Soup 97

Cheesy Vegetable Soup 98

East Coast–Style Chowder 101

Roasted Butternut Squash Soup 102

Cream of Mushroom Soup 104

Sesame Mixed Vegetables 106

Thai Coconut Rice 107

Sweet Sriracha Roasted Cauliflower 109

Ginger-Glazed Carrots 110

Broccoli with Cheese Sauce 113

Perfectly Photogenic Roasted Veggies 114

Cheesy Toasted Garlic Bread 117

Roasted Mini Potatoes with Basil Cream 118

Super-Fluffy Mashed Potatoes 120

Cajun-Spiced Wedges 121

Baked Sweet Potato Fries with
Curry Mayo 123

Crispy Baked Onion Rings 124

SANDWICHES, WRAPS & SALADS 127

Buffalo Chickpea Wraps 128

Gooey Grilled Cheese Sandwiches 130

Sweet Sriracha Cauliflower Wraps 131

BBQ Tofu–Stuffed Pita Pockets 133

Chickpea Tuna Pita Pockets 134

Strawberry Spinach Salad with
Buttermilk-Style Dressing 135

Sweet Potato Salad with Spiced
Maple Dressing 136

Thai Spiral Noodle Salad 139

Basil, Tomato and Parmesan
Pasta Salad 140

Broccoli Quinoa Salad with
Creamy Cashew Dressing 143

Simple Apple and Kale Salad 144

Summery Quinoa salad 147

Caesar Salad with Garlicky Croutons 148

MAINS 151

Saucy Seitan Sandwiches 152

Spicy "Sausage" Tacos 155

Untraditional "Chicken" Parmesan 156

Black Bean and Corn Tacos 159

Lentil Chili 160

Hawaiian-ish Pizza 163

Caprese Pizza 164

Chickpea, Lentil and Sweet
Potato Curry 165

Mac and Cheese Bake 166

Maple Curry Penne 169

Red Pepper Fettuccini 170

Lemon Asparagus Risotto 173

Sweet Chili Tofu and Rice Bowls 174

Spaghetti Squash Pad Thai 177

Vegetable Fried Rice 178

Dragon Noodles 181

SWEETS 183

My Favorite Banana Bread 184

Carrot Cake with Cream Cheese
Frosting 187

Fast and Fluffy No-Rise Cinnamon
Rolls 189

Chewy Chocolate Chip Cookies 193

Chocolate Walnut Cookie Bars 194

No-Bake Brownie Bites 196

Deep Dish Apple Pie with
Caramel Sauce 197

Edible Cookie Dough 200

Gingerbread Cake with Caramel
Sauce 203

Chocolate Raspberry Mini Cakes 204

Rosalie's Peach Cobbler 207

Strawberry Shortcakes 208

Chocolate Zucchini Cupcakes
with Mocha Frosting 211

Vanilla Birthday Cupcakes 214

Marble Freezer Fudge 217

ACKNOWLEDGMENTS 219
INDEX 221

Introduction

Cooking and eating are two of my favorite pastimes. But, to be honest, I really don't love spending tons of time in the kitchen. My favorite kind of meals are the ones that are easy and simple and taste absolutely delicious despite putting in minimal effort. Every time I follow a recipe, I ask myself, "How can I simplify this?" One of my biggest annoyances while cooking is trying to make a recipe that has an unnecessarily long and complicated ingredients list and an even more complicated set of instructions. There is always a fear that, after spending money and time on a fancy recipe, it might turn out to be a total flop. I like to avoid that by staying away from "fancy" ingredients and extra steps that might be confusing. I want you to be able to flip through this book and make the recipes without a struggle. I also want you to be able to find the ingredients at your grocery store and not have to go to a specialty health food store. But make no mistake — just because I keep a budget in mind when creating recipes, it doesn't mean the food is boring, plain or bland. I'm here to show you that you can eat on a budget and still cook incredibly delicious and fun plant-based meals that make you look and feel amazing.

Like most other areas of my life, the contents of this book focus on balance. I absolutely love fruits, veggies, grains, starches, nuts and seeds; there seem to be endless combinations of even the simplest ingredients that never get old. However, there is also no denying that I LOVE treats of all kinds — chocolate, cookies, pies, cakes . . . the list goes on. I grew up in a family that viewed cooking as a way to show love for each other and to enjoy one another's company. Recipes were passed down from grandmothers to mothers and then to me, and I am so happy to be able to veganize them and share them with you. There is a mix of everything in this book: family recipes, my own favorite recipes, some of my most popular YouTube recipes, and a few happy accidents that turned out even more amazing than what I intended in the first place!

Going vegan single-handedly changed the course of my life. In my first year of college, I developed some tough undiagnosed digestive problems. Throughout that year I saw both doctors and naturopaths and underwent tests and elimination diets. After discovering that lactose intolerance was causing some of my digestive issues, I decided to give up dairy. The next year I gave up red meat, then all meat, and eventually fish and eggs. My transition to a vegan diet and lifestyle was slow, but it soon became one of my biggest passions.

In 2015 I started a food blog and a YouTube channel called Liv's Healthy Life to document the food I was eating and all the fun recipes I had tried out. In the summer of 2016 one of my YouTube videos, "Vegan School Lunch Ideas in a Bento Box," went viral and people began finding my channel by the thousands. In a few months it grew from 4,000 subscribers to 250,000 and I was doing YouTube full-time while finishing my communications degree. Now with more than 650,000 subscribers, my YouTube channel has become just Liv B and encompasses all things vegan.

I wouldn't be where I am today without everyone who has ever watched my videos, made a recipe or supported me in some way. Having the opportunity to create this book and share these recipes with you has been a dream come true. I hope it inspires you to get in the kitchen and start creating some really great vegan food.

All my love!
— Liv

Getting Started

Whether you have been vegan for a while or are just interested in trying out some delicious plant-based recipes, this section has the info you'll need to know when cooking from this book.

Hopefully you are pumped up and inspired to get in the kitchen and start making some amazing vegan food. But before we get to that (and we will, soon!) there are a few basics we need to cover. If you've never cooked before or never made a vegan recipe, you'll want to read through this section to get the goods on vegan cooking and baking before diving into the recipes. Don't be scared — all the recipes in this book are straightforward and simple, but it's always good to be prepared and know the basics.

Tips for Being Vegan on a Budget

For me these days, being vegan on a budget has never been easier. But there are definitely some rules I follow and tricks I have learned over the years to get the most out of my money while still enjoying all the delicious foods I love.

COOK AT HOME: This one is easy now that you have this book! Cooking meals at home is a no-brainer if you are on a budget. It's no secret that eating out in restaurants is always more expensive than making your own food. The good news is, I love making restaurant-worthy meals in the comfort of my own kitchen. I have included tons of them in this book, such as Avocado Fried Toast, Maple Curry Penne, Saucy Seitan Sandwiches, Dragon Noodles, Caesar Salad with Garlicky Croutons and Deep-Dish Apple Pie with Caramel Sauce.

BUY IN BULK: Bulk food stores or even the bulk section at your grocery store is a lifesaver for staples such as nuts, seeds, flour and even grains like rice and quinoa. Buying in bulk cuts down on cost, since you're typically not spending extra for packaging or a brand name.

MAKE RECIPES THAT USE SIMILAR INGREDIENTS: I tend to use a lot of similar ingredients in my recipes, which will save you money because you won't have to restock your entire kitchen every time you make a recipe from this book. Finding recipes that call for the same produce or pantry staples will allow you to use what you have and reduce the chances that you'll be left with a ton of half-used ingredients that may go to waste at the end of the week.

USE LEFTOVERS: Leftovers are the best! Make sure you have reusable containers to keep leftovers properly stored so they last. Freezing leftovers is also a great way to cut down on food waste, and it gives you quick, easy-access meals for those busy days or weeks when you are short on time.

Stocking Your Kitchen

While I tried to make these recipes as accessible and unfussy as possible, there are some kitchen tools and pantry staples you will want to have on hand, or at least be aware of going forward. I'm all about multiuse tools and making do with what you have, but I've included a list of the kitchen tools used in this book, as well as pantry staples, so you can get stocked up and be ready to cook.

Kitchen Tools

I try to be minimalistic when it comes to kitchen tools. That being said, having a few good-quality items will make your life easier. I've recommended a few below that will help you make the recipes in this book, and experiment with your own cooking and baking!

Blender (regular or high-powered)

Can opener

Electric mixer

Food processor

Frying pan

Jars and food storage containers

Large pot

Medium pot

Rimmed baking sheets

Rolling pin

Spatula

Strainer

Wooden spoons

8-inch (20 cm) square metal baking pan

9- by 5-inch (23 by 12.5 cm) metal loaf pan

Pantry Staples

These pantry staples are great to keep on hand because they are used in recipes throughout the book. I make sure to have them stocked up so I'm prepared anytime a recipe craving hits!

DRY PANTRY STAPLES

All-purpose flour (I use unbleached in a few recipes)

Cocoa powder (unsweetened)

Chia seeds

Ground flax seeds

Nutritional yeast

Nuts (cashews, almonds, pecans, walnuts)

Oats (quick-cooking and large-flake/old-fashioned)

Pasta (penne, bowties, fettuccini, spaghetti, lasagna, macaroni)

Quinoa

Red lentils

Rice (white and brown)

Sesame seeds

Vanilla extract

CANNED AND JARRED PANTRY STAPLES

Almond butter

Coconut oil

Diced tomatoes

Full-fat coconut milk

Beans (chickpeas and black beans)

Lentils

Olive oil

Pure maple syrup

Soy sauce or tamari

Tahini

Tomato salsa

Tomato sauce

HERBS AND SPICES

Chili powder

Curry powder

Dried basil

Dried oregano

Garlic powder

Ground cinnamon

Ground ginger

Ground turmeric

Hot pepper flakes

Onion powder

Paprika

Pepper

Salt

Two Important How-To's

There are a two how-to's that will help you when making some recipes from this book — how to press tofu and how to soak cashews. Since both of these techniques come up throughout the book, I've included step-by-step instructions here for you to refer to when making a recipe that calls for either.

HOW TO PRESS TOFU

Tofu comes packaged in water and, like a sponge, it can hold a lot of it. Pressing the water out of the tofu makes room for it to absorb the flavors you want, and it also improves the texture by making it less soggy. Pressing tofu is actually quite easy:

1. Lay a clean dish towel on a baking sheet and cover it with a few paper towels.

2. Slice open the tofu and discard the water from the package. Place the tofu on the paper towels. Put a few more paper towels on top of the tofu, followed by another dish towel.

3. Place a heavy object on top of everything (if you are using a book, add another baking sheet first so it doesn't get wet).

4. Let stand at room temperature for 30 minutes or up to 2 hours. Proceed with your recipe as directed.

HOW TO SOAK CASHEWS

Puréed cashews are often used in this book to add creaminess to recipes such as sauces. Soaking cashews makes them soft and easier to blend, which is why I recommend it, especially if you don't have a high-powered blender. Here's all you need to do:

1. Put the cashews in a bowl and cover them with hot water.

2. Let stand at room temperature for a minimum of 1 hour or up to 12 hours.

3. Drain and use as directed.

If you are super-short on time, you can cook the cashews in a pot of boiling water for 10 minutes, then drain and use as directed.

Sample Menus

Owning a book of recipes is great, but knowing which ones are tasty and convenient to serve together, and for what sort of occasion, is a whole other challenge. In this section I have created some menus with recipes from this book that I think will be perfect for various occasions. I have included a menu for a holiday dinner, a weekend dinner party, brunch with your best friends and an outdoor summer meal. These are occasions when I typically look to make something extra special, and these menus always do the trick!

Holiday Dinner

Holiday dinners are often a point of concern for people who are looking to go vegan, since traditional holiday meals usually consist of a lot of meat and dairy-heavy dishes. These recipes combine some classic holiday flavors and make an excellent spread for a vegan dinner table.

Sliceable Seitan (page 25) or Crispy Tofu Dippers (page 69)

Super-Fluffy Mashed Potatoes (page 120)

Veggie Gravy (page 13)

Broccoli with Cheese Sauce (page 113)

Ginger-Glazed Carrots (page 110) or Perfectly Photogenic Roasted Veggies (page 114)

Gingerbread with Caramel Sauce (page 203) or Deep Dish Apple Pie with Caramel Sauce (page 197)

Weekend Dinner Party

My favorite dinner parties are ones where everyone sits around the table drinking wine, telling stories and feasting on comfort food. Whether your guests are vegan or not, I know they will enjoy these vegan versions of comforting classics!

Caesar Salad with Garlicky Croutons (page 148)

Cheesy Toasted Garlic Bread (page 117)

Red Pepper Fettuccini (page 170)

No-Bake Brownie Bites (page 196) or Chocolate Walnut Cookie Bars (page 194)

Brunch with Friends

I love having friends over for brunch. Since I can never choose between sweet or savory for breakfast, I enjoy being able to cook a bunch of both types of food so everyone can have a little taste of everything.

Tropical Green Smoothie (page 35)

Crispy Breakfast Potatoes (page 55)

Mini Chocolate Lava Pancakes (page 51)

Chickpea Scramble (page 61)

Overnight Muesli (page 40)

Outdoor Summer Meal

This menu is perfect for enjoying outdoors on a warm summer evening. The saucy barbecue-flavored seitan sandwiches are sure to be a hit, and the fruit-based appetizer and dessert add the best summertime vibes to the meal.

Spicy Mango Salsa (page 78)

Five-Minute Guacamole (page 78)

Saucy Seitan Sandwiches (page 152)

Simple Apple and Kale Salad (page 144)

Chocolate-Dipped Fruit Pops (page 86)

Icons

You will notice three icons that pop up in recipes throughout this book:

GLUTEN-FREE: This icon identifies recipes that are suitable for those of you who suffer from celiac disease or who need to avoid gluten.

GREAT FOR GATHERINGS: Tested by my own friends and family, these recipes are crowd-pleasers and easy to make in large quantities.

PORTABLE: There isn't always time to make and eat your meals at home. These recipes are great for taking with you on the go in a reusable container or jar.

I hope this section has helped give you a general overview of how to use this book so you get the most out of it. If I have any last words of advice for you, it's to remember not to take things too seriously. Cooking is a sometimes messy endeavor that has a learning curve, but you will only get better with practice. Try to approach these recipes with an open mind and a light heart and I have a feeling you will do just fine. Now go forth and start cooking!

Staples & Sauces

Cashew Milk Two Ways

Most nut milk recipes require hours of soaking plus straining at the end to remove the pulp. These two recipes take much less time — one doesn't even require soaking! —and neither produces any waste.

USING A HIGH-POWERED BLENDER

• MAKES 2 CUPS (500 ML) • • 5 MINUTES (PLUS 1 HOUR FOR SOAKING) •

½ cup (125 mL) raw cashews

1 cup (250 mL) hot water

2 cups (500 mL) cold water, divided

2 tsp (10 mL) pure maple syrup or agave nectar

1. Soak the cashews in the hot water in a medium bowl for 1 hour. Drain.

2. Combine the cashews and ½ cup (125 mL) cold water in a high-powered blender; blend on high speed for about 2 minutes, until completely smooth, with a cream-like consistency.

3. Add 1½ cups (375 mL) cold water and the maple syrup; blend on high speed for 30 seconds to 1 minute, until completely smooth.

4. Store in a glass jar with a lid (I like mason jars) for up to 5 days in the fridge. The milk will separate in the fridge as it sits, so shake well before consuming.

USING A REGULAR BLENDER

• MAKES 2 CUPS (500 ML) • • 5 MINUTES •

2 tbsp (30 mL) cashew butter or almond butter

2 cups (500 mL) cold water

2 tsp (10 mL) pure maple syrup or agave nectar

1. Combine the cashew butter, cold water and maple syrup in a blender; blend on high speed for about 1 minute, until completely smooth.

2. Store in a glass jar with a lid (I like mason jars) for up to 5 days in the fridge. The milk will separate in the fridge as it sits, so shake well before consuming.

My Tip

The milk can sometimes be a bit warm right after blending. It is fine to use warm in oatmeal or coffee, but if you plan to drink it straight, I suggest chilling it in the fridge for 2 hours.

Marinara Sauce

• MAKES APPROX. 3 CUPS (750 ML) • · TIME: 20 MINUTES •

I was always a bit intimated by marinara sauce because I thought it would be difficult to achieve that restaurant quality at home. One winter evening, I decided to try my luck making my own marinara and it quickly became a staple for delicious pasta at home. I like to change it up by adding vegetables such as pan-fried zucchini and mushrooms, but the base sauce always stays the same — it's just so easy to make and tastes fresh and delicious.

1 tbsp (15 mL) olive oil

½ medium Spanish onion, chopped

1 can (28 ounce/796 mL) no-salt-added crushed tomatoes

1 cup (250 mL) no-salt-added tomato sauce

2 tsp (10 mL) organic cane sugar

1 tsp (5 mL) dried basil

½ tsp (2 mL) salt

¼ tsp (1 mL) black pepper

Blender

1. Heat a medium frying pan over medium heat. Add the oil and onion and cook, stirring occasionally, for 5 minutes, until translucent.

2. Meanwhile, add the crushed tomatoes to the blender and pulse about 5 times, until slightly smooth.

3. Add the blended tomatoes, tomato sauce, sugar, basil, salt and pepper to the frying pan and stir to combine. Reduce heat to medium-low and simmer, stirring frequently, for 10 minutes to allow flavors to meld.

4. Serve immediately or store in an airtight container in the fridge for up to 4 days.

My Tip

This sauce can be frozen for up to 4 months. To defrost, remove from the freezer and refrigerate overnight or for up to 24 hours. When ready to eat, heat in a medium pot over low heat for about 10 minutes, stirring frequently, until heated through.

Veggie Gravy

Something that is often overlooked at holiday dinners is a vegan gravy. Most traditional gravy is made using animal-based broth, which means if you are vegan you will be eating your mashed potatoes plain. I don't want that to happen to you! I always make a batch of this gravy and bring it to holiday dinners so the host doesn't have to do any extra work and I can still enjoy my mashed potatoes with gravy.

1 tbsp (15 mL) vegan butter

¼ cup (60 mL) finely chopped onion

2 cups (500 mL) vegetable broth

1 tbsp (15 mL) reduced-sodium soy sauce (optional)

3 tbsp (45 mL) cornstarch

3 tbsp (45 mL) water

Salt and black pepper

1. Melt the vegan butter in a medium pot over medium heat. Add the onion and cook, stirring occasionally, for about 5 minutes, until translucent.

2. Add the vegetable broth and soy sauce (if using) and bring to a light simmer.

3. Meanwhile, stir together the cornstarch and water in a small bowl or cup.

4. Whisking constantly, add the cornstarch to the pot; continue whisking for 1 to 2 minutes, until thickened. Season to taste with salt and pepper. Remove from heat and serve immediately or let cool and store in an airtight container in the fridge for up to 2 days (see My Tip for reheating instructions).

My Tip

Reheat the gravy on the stove in a medium pot over medium heat for about 8 minutes, stirring frequently, until smooth and heated through.

Orange Almond Butter Sauce

• MAKES ½ CUP (125 ML), ABOUT 2 SERVINGS ⑂ TIME: 5 MINUTES •

This thick and creamy sauce is perfect over steamed veggies and quinoa or rice noodles and tofu. Not only does it taste delicious, it turns an otherwise basic meal into one that is luxurious and flavorful. You'll be able to put dinner on the table in no time. I double the recipe when I have more people coming over or want to have leftovers.

¼ cup (60 mL) creamy almond butter

3 tbsp (45 mL) reduced-sodium soy sauce

¼ cup (60 mL) pulp-free orange juice

3 tbsp (45 mL) brown sugar

½ tsp (2 mL) Sriracha sauce

1. Whisk together the almond butter, soy sauce, orange juice, brown sugar and Sriracha sauce in a medium bowl until smooth and creamy. Use immediately or store in an airtight container in the fridge for up to 1 week.

Creamy Hummus Salad Dressing

This is one of my go-to dressings for a quick salad because it's a great way to use up that last little bit of hummus before it goes bad. I like it on a simple salad made with greens, cucumber, tomato and shredded carrot, or any other veg you've got in the back of the fridge that's almost past its peak. It's the type of meal that can really help cut down on food waste.

½ cup (125 mL) hummus

1 tbsp (15 mL) freshly squeezed lemon juice

2 tsp (10 mL) pure maple syrup or agave nectar

2 tbsp (30 mL) water

1. Whisk together the hummus, lemon juice, maple syrup and water in a small bowl until smooth. Serve immediately or store in an airtight container in the fridge for up to 3 days.

Thai Peanut Sauce

• MAKES ½ CUP (125 ML), ABOUT 2 SERVINGS   TIME: 5 MINUTES •

Finding vegan food at Thai restaurants can be challenging because of the amount of seafood and other animal products used in the cuisine, but making Thai-inspired food at home is actually very simple. This peanut sauce combines all the great Thai flavors you crave but is completely plant-based. I like to eat it warm or cold, and it's the perfect addition to noodle bowls, stir-fries and salads. It also makes a great dipping sauce for Best-Ever Tofu Cubes (page 22).

⅓ cup (75 mL) creamy peanut butter or almond butter

3 tbsp (45 mL) reduced-sodium soy sauce

3 tbsp (45 mL) brown sugar or pure maple syrup

2 tbsp (30 mL) freshly squeezed lime juice

¼ tsp (1 mL) garlic powder

½ tsp (2 mL) Sriracha sauce

1. Whisk together the peanut butter, soy sauce, brown sugar, lime juice, garlic powder and Sriracha sauce in a small bowl until smooth. Use immediately or store in an airtight container in the fridge for up to 5 days.

My Tip

Substitute sunflower seed butter or tahini for a nut-free version. If you want the sauce to be thinner, add about 2 tbsp (30 mL) warm water and whisk again until smooth.

Vegan "Honey Mustard" Dip

• MAKES ½ CUP (125 ML) • • TIME: 5 MINUTES •

This is a really great multipurpose "honey" dip that goes well with tons of dishes, such as my Crispy Tofu Dippers (page 69), and it's also super tasty as a spread on wraps and sandwiches. I hosted a Super Bowl party this year and served it alongside vegan sausage rolls. My friends not only devoured all of it, they asked me to make more!

¼ cup (60 mL) vegan mayonnaise

3 tbsp (45 mL) Dijon mustard

3 tbsp (45 mL) pure maple syrup or agave nectar

1. Whisk together the vegan mayonnaise, Dijon mustard and maple syrup in a small bowl until smooth. Serve immediately or store in an airtight container in the fridge for up to 5 days.

Spicy Lime Mayo

I love the tangy, spicy flavor of this mayo on Black Bean and Corn Tacos (page 159), or as a dip for my Cajun-Spiced Wedges (page 121). I know spiciness is a highly personal matter and that some people can tolerate more heat than others. This mayo is on the milder side, so if you enjoy heat, be sure to add more Sriracha sauce.

½ cup (125 mL) vegan mayonnaise

1 tbsp (15 mL) freshly squeezed lime juice

1 tsp (5 mL) Sriracha sauce or hot sauce

1. Whisk together the vegan mayonnaise, lime juice and Sriracha sauce until smooth. Serve immediately or store in an airtight container in the fridge for up to 1 week.

Cheese Sauce

I spent *a lot* of time perfecting a vegan cheese sauce recipe that was as indulgent and cheesy-tasting as its non-vegan counterpart. As an added bonus, this recipe is healthier than a traditional cheese sauce because the base is made from potato and carrot.

⅓ cup (75 mL) raw cashews

1 large russet potato, peeled and cubed

1 medium carrot, peeled and chopped

Water

¼ cup (60 mL) nutritional yeast

2 tbsp (30 mL) freshly squeezed lemon juice

¼ tsp (1 mL) Dijon mustard

½ tsp (2 mL) salt

¼ tsp (1 mL) garlic powder

High-powered blender or regular blender

1. If you are not using a high-powered blender, cover the cashews with very hot water in a bowl and soak for 1 hour. If you have a high-powered blender, proceed to Step 2.

2. Place the potato and carrot in a medium pot and add enough water to cover. Boil for about 12 minutes over high heat, until tender. Drain and rinse with cold water until the vegetables have cooled completely.

3. Drain the cashews, if necessary. Add the cooked potato and carrot, cashews, ⅓ cup (75 mL) water, nutritional yeast, lemon juice, Dijon mustard, salt and garlic powder to the blender. Blend on high speed for about 1 to 2 minutes, until completely smooth.

4. **TO SERVE IMMEDIATELY:** Pour the sauce into a medium pot over medium-low heat; stir constantly for about 5 minutes, until heated through. Serve. **TO STORE:** Transfer to an airtight container or jar and store in the fridge for up to 4 days.

My Tip

For a more budget-friendly and nut-free option, omit the cashews. To get a rich and creamy texture without the nuts, use 1/3 cup (75 mL) full-fat coconut milk instead of water.

Vegan Ricotta Two Ways

This vegan ricotta can be used anywhere you would use dairy ricotta. I love it on top of Famous Lasagna Soup (page 94), spread over bagels or crackers, and to make super Gooey Grilled Cheese Sandwiches (page 130). I have provided two options, one that is soy-free and one that is nut-free, so everyone can enjoy the wonder that is plant-based ricotta cheese.

ALMOND RICOTTA (USING A HIGH-POWERED BENDER)

• MAKES APPROX. 1½ CUPS (375 ML) • • TIME: 5 MINUTES •

¾ cup (175 mL) water, divided

1½ cups (375 mL) slivered almonds

2 tbsp (30 mL) nutritional yeast

2 tbsp (30 mL) freshly squeezed lemon juice

½ tsp (2 mL) salt

⅛ tsp (0.5 mL) garlic powder

1. Combine ½ cup (125 mL) water, almonds, nutritional yeast, lemon juice, salt and garlic powder in the blender. Blend on high speed for about 4 minutes, stopping the motor to scrape down the sides of the jar as necessary. Add the remaining water 2 tbsp (30 mL) at a time; blend until mostly smooth and no large chunks remain.

2. Use immediately or store in an airtight container in the fridge for up to 5 days.

TOFU RICOTTA (USING A REGULAR BLENDER)

12 oz (375 g) firm tofu

3 tbsp (45 mL) nutritional yeast

2 tbsp (30 mL) freshly squeezed lemon juice

½ tsp (2 mL) salt

1 garlic clove

½ tsp (2 mL) onion powder

1 to 2 tbsp (15 to 30 mL) olive oil, divided

1. Combine the tofu, nutritional yeast, lemon juice, salt, garlic, onion powder and 1 tbsp (15 mL) oil in the blender. Blend on high speed for 1 to 2 minutes, until somewhat smooth and the texture resembles ricotta cheese. Add the remaining 1 tbsp (15 mL) oil if necessary to help blend.

2. Use immediately or store in an airtight container in the fridge for up to 5 days.

Best-Ever Tofu Cubes

• SERVES 4 • • TIME: 25 MINUTES •

This tofu recipe was actually perfected by my mom. She always claimed she hated tofu until I gave her some pointers on how to make it crispier. She has now made it often enough that she nails the perfect crispiness every time. You can use these tofu cubes as added protein in many recipes, but my current favorite is Sweet Chili Tofu and Rice Bowls (page 174).

12 oz (375 g) firm tofu

⅓ cup (75 mL) cornstarch (approx.)

3 tbsp (45 mL) vegetable oil

1. Place the tofu on a clean, folded dishtowel. Place another clean folded dishtowel on top, followed by a large pot or frying pan. Let stand for 5 to 10 minutes while the towels absorb the moisture.

2. Remove dishtowels and cut the tofu into bite-size cubes.

3. Place the cornstarch in a medium bowl, then add the tofu cubes and toss to coat.

4. Heat a large frying pan over medium-high heat. Add the oil and heat for about 1 minute, until shimmering. Add the tofu and cook for about 8 minutes or until crispy and golden on one side. Flip and continue cooking, turning occasionally, for 7 minutes more, until crispy and golden.

5. Remove from heat and use immediately.

My Tip

Because these tofu cubes are fried, they don't reheat well. I suggest making only as much as you need. This recipe is great halved!

Seitan "Sausage" Crumbles

• SERVES 4 ♥ TIME: 20 MINUTES •

Many seitan recipes call for a long list of ingredients and lengthy preparation time, which is understandable — it's not easy to recreate meat! However, this recipe takes no more than 20 minutes from start to finish and yields a super-delicious mock sausage that can be used in many dishes that require crumbled meat. Try it in Spicy "Sausage" Tacos (page 155) or on my Hawaiian-ish Pizza (page 163).

1 cup (250 mL) vital wheat gluten	¼ tsp (1 mL) garlic powder
3 tbsp (45 mL) nutritional yeast	⅓ cup (75 mL) water
½ tsp (2 mL) salt	3 tbsp (45 mL) ketchup
2 tsp (10 mL) chili powder	3 tbsp (45 mL) apple cider vinegar
¼ tsp (1 mL) cayenne pepper	¼ cup (60 mL) vegetable oil, divided

1. Whisk together the vital wheat gluten, nutritional yeast, salt, chili powder, cayenne pepper and garlic powder in a medium bowl.

2. Whisk together the water, ketchup, vinegar and 2 tbsp (30 mL) oil in a separate small bowl.

3. Pour the ketchup mixture into the vital wheat gluten mixture and combine, using your hands, until small crumbles form that resemble ground meat. (If the pieces are too large they will be chewy and gummy.)

4. Add the remaining 2 tbsp (30 mL) oil to a frying pan over medium heat and heat for 45 seconds. Add the seitan crumbles to the pan and cook, stirring frequently, for about 8 minutes, until crispy and golden brown. Use immediately or store in an airtight container in the fridge for up to 3 days.

My Tip

Vital wheat gluten is the natural protein found in wheat. It is almost pure gluten and is typically found in the "natural/organic" section of grocery stores or at specialty food stores. Since vital wheat gluten is a non-perishable packaged ingredient, it is easy to order online if you cannot find it locally.

Sliceable Seitan

• SERVES 4 ♡ TIME: 1½ HOURS •

Seitan, also referred to as "wheat meat," is a great meat substitute. On its own it has a fairly mild flavor, which is why I like to spice it up with sauces and seasonings. Check out my Saucy Seitan Sandwiches (page 152) for a delicious and fun way to use this recipe.

1½ cups (375 mL) vital wheat gluten (see My Tip, page 24)

1 tsp (5 mL) dried oregano

½ tsp (2 mL) salt

½ tsp (2 mL) onion powder

¼ tsp (1 mL) garlic powder

1 tbsp (15 mL) nutritional yeast (optional)

4 cups (1 L) vegan chicken-flavored broth or vegetable broth, divided

2 tbsp (30 mL) tahini

2 tbsp (30 mL) olive oil

8- by 4-inch (20 by 10 cm) loaf pan

1. Preheat the oven to 375°F (190°C).

2. Whisk together the vital wheat gluten, oregano, salt, onion powder, garlic powder and nutritional yeast in a large bowl.

3. Whisk together 1¼ cups (300 mL) broth, tahini and oil in a medium bowl. Pour the broth mixture into the vital wheat gluten mixture and stir until a ball of dough forms. Knead the dough in the bowl for about 1 minute, until it becomes firmer and more elastic. Using your hands, form the dough into a log approximately 6 inches (15 cm) long and 2½ inches (6 cm) in diameter.

4. Place the dough log in the loaf pan and cover with the remaining broth.

5. Bake in the preheated oven for 40 minutes. Remove from the oven, flip over and bake for another 20 minutes, until firm. Remove from the pan and place on a plate or cutting board to cool slightly. Discard the broth.

6. Slice and serve warm or let cool completely, then transfer to a resealable freezer bag and store in the fridge for up to 4 days or the freezer for 3 months. If frozen, thaw in the fridge overnight prior to use; reheat in the microwave on Medium until warm.

Vanilla Almond Butter

• MAKES 1½ CUPS (375 ML) • • TIME: 20 MINUTES •

I use almond butter throughout this book. I often sub this vanilla version in recipes that call for regular almond butter, to add a bit of sweetness, like my Almond Butter Toast with Caramelized Bananas (page 49), Warm Apples and Almond Butter Bowls (page 48) or my Berry Smoothie Bowls (page 36). It also makes a delicious filling, healthy and simple snack-on-the-go served alongside apple slices for dipping.

3 cups (750 mL) raw almonds

1 tsp (5 mL) vanilla extract

1 tbsp (15 mL) pure maple syrup or agave nectar

1 vanilla bean, split and scraped (optional; see My Tip)

Food processor

1. Place the almonds in the food processor and process for about 15 minutes, stopping the motor every few minutes to scrape down the sides of the bowl as necessary, until very smooth. (They can take a while to process, but don't give up! The nut butter will appear thick for a while until the oils are released, and then it will get to a nice runny, spreadable consistency. You'll notice that change around the 10- to 12-minute mark.)

2. Add the vanilla extract, maple syrup and vanilla bean seeds (if using); process for 1 minute, until combined.

3. Let stand in the food processor for about 10 minutes, until cooled slightly. Serve immediately or store in an airtight container in the fridge for up to 2 weeks.

My Tip

To remove vanilla bean seeds from the pod, split the bean lengthwise, using a sharp paring knife. Working with one half at a time, hold the end against the cutting board and use the knife to scrape out the seeds.

Caramel Sauce

• MAKES 1½ CUPS (375 ML) • • TIME: 15 MINUTES •

This recipe from my grandmother wasn't originally vegan, but with a few simple changes it became a super-delicious vegan caramel sauce, perfect for topping Fast and Fluffy No-Rise Cinnamon Rolls (page 189), Deep Dish Apple Pie (page 197) and Gingerbread Cake (page 203).

3 tbsp (45 mL) cornstarch

2 tbsp (30 mL) water

1½ cups (375 mL) boiling water

¼ cup (60 mL) lightly packed brown sugar

¼ cup (60 mL) organic cane sugar

2 tbsp (30 mL) light (fancy) molasses

⅛ tsp (0.5 mL) ground nutmeg

2 tsp (10 mL) vanilla extract

1½ tbsp (22 mL) vegan butter

1. Whisk together the cornstarch and 2 tbsp (30 mL) water in a small pot, until smooth.

2. Add the boiling water, brown sugar, cane sugar, molasses, nutmeg, vanilla and vegan butter; stir to combine.

3. Bring to a simmer over medium heat and cook, stirring, for about 5 minutes, until the sauce thickens. Use immediately or store in an airtight container in the fridge for up to 4 days.

My Tip

To reheat the sauce, add to a small pot and heat over medium-low heat for 5 minutes, stirring frequently, until smooth and heated through. You can also add it to a microwave-safe bowl and microwave on Medium, pausing to stir occasionally, until hot.

Breakfast & Brunch

Strawberry Citrus Smoothie

• SERVES 2 • • TIME: 5 MINUTES •

Smoothies are a go-to breakfast for me. They are quick to make and super nutritious, and they can be different every day, depending on what you put in them. Since this is a light smoothie, I like to have it along with something else, such as Chickpea Scramble (page 61) or pancakes.

1½ cups (375 mL) orange juice

2 tbsp (30 mL) ground flax seeds

1 cup (250 mL) frozen strawberries

1 frozen banana, chopped

Blender

1. Pour the orange juice into the blender. Add the ground flax seeds, strawberries and banana. Blend on high speed for 1 minute, until smooth. Pour into 2 glasses and serve.

My Tip

If you are looking to make this smoothie a bit more filling, try adding a serving of protein powder or 2 tbsp (30 mL) chia seeds before blending. Both options will give it more staying power and keep you fuller longer.

Pre-Workout Berry Smoothie

• SERVES 1 • ⊛ ⊙ • TIME: 5 MINUTES •

I don't like working out on a full stomach, so having a light smoothie beforehand gives me just enough energy without weighing me down. You can typically find bags of mixed berries in the freezer section of your grocery store.

½ cup (125 mL) water

½ cup (125 mL) orange juice

1 tsp (5 mL) chia seeds

½ cup (125 mL) frozen mixed berries

1 frozen banana, chopped

Blender

1. Pour the water and orange juice into the blender. Add the chia seeds, frozen berries and banana. Blend on high speed for about 1 minute, until smooth. Pour into a glass and serve.

Post-Workout Choco Smoothie

• SERVES 1 • ⊛ ⊙ • TIME: 5 MINUTES •

If I don't have a pre-workout smoothie, I always have a post-workout smoothie. I use a chocolate-flavored protein powder here because it adds extra chocolatey goodness.

1 cup (250 mL) chocolate almond milk

1 serving vegan chocolate protein powder

1 tbsp (15 mL) ground flax seeds

1 ripe banana

½ cup (125 mL) frozen blueberries

½ cup (125 mL) frozen strawberries

Blender

1. Pour the almond milk into the blender. Add the protein powder, ground flax seeds, banana, frozen blueberries and frozen strawberries. Blend on high speed for 1 minute, until smooth. Pour into a glass and serve.

Tropical Green Smoothie

• SERVES 2 •   • TIME: 5 MINUTES •

Back when green smoothies were just starting to gain popularity, I was really skeptical about trying them. I was convinced that putting greens in a smoothie would make it taste like salad. Since then I've played around with variations and came up with this recipe, which tastes like a tropical cocktail but also has a good amount of greens. It is so beautiful and vibrant, and it makes you feel that way when you drink it!

1½ cups (375 mL) coconut water or water

1 tbsp (15 mL) chia seeds

1 cup (250 mL) baby spinach

1 cup (250 mL) frozen mango chunks

½ cup (125 mL) frozen peach slices or frozen pineapple chunks

2 ripe bananas

Blender

1. Pour the coconut water into the blender. Add the chia seeds, spinach, frozen mango, frozen peaches and bananas. Blend on high speed for about 1 minute, until smooth. Pour into 2 glasses and serve.

My Tip

You can also turn this into a smoothie bowl. First, thicken the smoothie by using frozen bananas instead of fresh. Then top it with 1 tbsp (15 mL) unsweetened coconut flakes and ½ cup (125 mL) fresh berries.

Berry Smoothie Bowls

· SERVES 2 · · TIME: 15 MINUTES ·

Some people really don't like the texture of smoothies or don't find them filling enough to get them through the morning. I serve those detractors this berry smoothie bowl, which is both delicious and nutritious. The berries are a great source of fiber and the chia seeds help thicken the texture and add essential omega-3s.

1 cup (250 mL) apple juice or orange juice

2 frozen bananas, chopped

2 tbsp (30 mL) chia seeds

1 cup (250 mL) frozen blueberries

1 cup (250 mL) frozen strawberries

Optional Toppings

Shredded coconut

2 tbsp (30 mL) cacao nibs

Spiced Coconut Granola (page 39) or store-bought

Almond butter or peanut butter

Fresh berries

Sliced banana

Blender

1. Place the apple juice, frozen bananas, chia seeds, frozen blueberries and frozen strawberries in the blender. Blend on high speed for about 1 minute, until smooth.

2. Divide between 2 bowls. Smooth out the top with a spoon and add shredded coconut, cacao nibs, granola, almond butter, fresh berries and/or sliced banana (if using).

Spiced Coconut Granola

• MAKES 2 CUPS (500 ML) ⩔ TIME: 35 MINUTES •

My kitchen always smells incredible whenever I'm baking granola. The nutty aroma of toasted coconut and pecans makes me want to eat it straight off the pan! It's great on its own or as a topping for my Berry Smoothie Bowls (page 36) and Warm Apples and Almond Butter Bowls (page 48).

1½ cups (375 mL) large-flake (old-fashioned) rolled oats

½ cup (125 mL) chopped pecans

½ cup (125 mL) unsweetened large coconut flakes or shredded coconut

½ tsp (2 mL) ground cinnamon

¼ cup (60 mL) coconut oil, melted

¼ cup (60 mL) pure maple syrup or agave nectar

Rimmed baking sheet, lined with parchment paper

1. Preheat the oven to 350°F (180°C).

2. Combine the oats, pecans, coconut flakes and cinnamon in a large bowl and stir to mix well.

3. Add the melted coconut oil and maple syrup and stir to combine.

4. Spread the mixture evenly on the prepared pan and bake in the preheated oven for 10 minutes. Remove from the oven, stir, and return to the oven. Bake for 8 more minutes — keeping an eye on it, since the edges have a tendency to burn — until golden brown.

5. Remove from the oven and let cool on the baking sheet for 20 minutes. Once completely cool, use immediately or store in an airtight container at room temperature for up to 10 days.

Overnight Muesli

Muesli is a lifesaver when things get hectic. It takes only a few minutes to make in the evening and you can wake up knowing your breakfast is already prepared. I like to top it with fresh fruit and nut butter, which I add just before eating. Try it with my Vanilla Almond Butter (page 26).

Muesli

1 cup (250 mL) quick-cooking rolled oats

2 tsp (10 mL) chia seeds

1½ cups (375 mL) unsweetened nondairy milk

2 tbsp (30 mL) pure maple syrup or agave nectar

¼ cup (60 mL) raisins

½ tsp (2 mL) ground cinnamon

For serving

1 ripe banana, sliced

½ cup (125 mL) fresh berries

¼ cup (60 mL) almond butter or peanut butter

1. Combine the oats, chia seeds, nondairy milk, maple syrup, raisins and cinnamon in a container or jar with a lid. Cover with the lid and refrigerate for at least 8 hours or overnight.

2. Transfer to 2 bowls (or leave in the container if you're on the move). Top each serving with banana slices, fresh berries and 1 tbsp (15 mL) almond butter.

My Tips

This muesli can be stored in an airtight container in the fridge for up to 3 days.

For the best results, don't top it with the fruit until right before eating.

Empty-Jar Overnight Oats

• SERVES 1 • ⬤ • TIME: 5 MINUTES (PLUS 8 HOURS FOR CHILLING) •

Do you ever find yourself wondering what to do with an almost empty container of nut butter, the one with a tiny amount lurking at the bottom and on the sides? It's not enough to make anything with, but it's enough that you don't want to just throw it out. This was a common occurrence for me until my friend Hannah showed me this trick, and now I can't wait until my jars are almost empty so I can make it.

½ cup (125 mL) quick-cooking rolled oats

1 cup (125 mL) unsweetened nondairy milk

1 tsp (5 mL) chia seeds

1 tsp (5 mL) ground cinnamon

1 tbsp (15 mL) pure maple syrup or agave nectar

One 12 oz to 1 lb (375 to 500 g) almost empty jar of nut butter

1. Add the oats, nondairy milk, chia seeds, cinnamon and maple syrup to the almost empty jar; stir to combine. Cover with the lid and transfer to the refrigerator for up to 8 hours. Stir well before serving.

My Tip

You can mix this up in a variety of ways. Try these flavor combinations:

Chocolate Overnight Oats: Stir 1 tbsp (15 mL) unsweetened cocoa powder, 1 tbsp (15 mL) additional nut butter and an extra 1 tbsp (15 mL) pure maple syrup or agave nectar into the oats. *Vanilla Blueberry Overnight Oats*: Stir ⅓ cup (75 mL) frozen blueberries, ½ tsp (2 mL) vanilla extract and ½ mashed ripe banana into the oats. *Chocolate Strawberry Overnight Oats*: Stir 1 tbsp (15 mL) strawberry jam and 1 tbsp (15 mL) vegan chocolate chips into the oats.

Blueberry Pie Oatmeal

Blueberry pie is my favorite dessert, so I decided to turn it into a breakfast recipe (and was more than happy to keep testing it until it was just right!). The key ingredients are the vanilla and cinnamon, warming flavors that make you feel cozy and comforted on a chilly morning.

¾ cup (175 mL) quick-cooking rolled oats

1½ cups (375 mL) water

1 cup (250 mL) frozen blueberries

2 tbsp (30 mL) water

1 tbsp (15 mL) organic cane sugar

1 tsp (5 mL) cornstarch

⅛ tsp (0.5 mL) ground cinnamon

¼ tsp (1 mL) vanilla extract

1. Combine the oats and water in a medium pot. Cook according to the package directions.

2. Combine the frozen blueberries, water, sugar, cornstarch, cinnamon and vanilla in a separate small pot. Simmer over medium heat for 5 minutes, stirring occasionally, until thickened slightly.

3. Evenly divide the cooked oats between 2 bowls. Pour the blueberry mixture overtop and serve.

Cinnamon Peach Oatmeal

• SERVES 2 ⱱ TIME: 10 MINUTES •

I pretty much wait all year for peach season so that I can make this oatmeal all the time. But sometimes in the dead of winter when the craving hits, I use frozen peaches and it still hits the spot. It's delicious with a sprinkle of granola and a drizzle of maple syrup.

¾ cup (175 mL) quick-cooking rolled oats

¾ cup (175 mL) water

¾ cup (175 mL) unsweetened nondairy milk

1 cup (250 mL) chopped peaches (thawed if frozen)

1 tbsp (15 mL) brown sugar

1 tsp (5 mL) ground cinnamon

½ tsp (2 mL) vanilla extract

Spiced Coconut Granola (page 39) or store-bought (optional)

Pure maple syrup (optional)

1. Combine the oats, water and nondairy milk in a medium pot. Cook according to the package directions.

2. Add the peaches, brown sugar, cinnamon and vanilla; stir to combine. Divide between 2 bowls and top with granola and maple syrup (if using).

Warm Apples and Almond Butter Bowls

• SERVES 2 • • TIME: 15 MINUTES •

I created this recipe back in my first semester of university. I had a very early class and an even earlier bus to catch, so I would cook some apples and layer them in a mason jar with almond butter and granola the night before and then quickly reheat it in the microwave before heading out the door in the morning. It was super portable — easy to eat on the bus or even in my first class! (If you're really short on time you can eat it cold.) On weekends, when I have more time, I like to eat this with a side of Crispy Breakfast Potatoes (page 55).

3 McIntosh apples, peeled and chopped

¼ cup (60 mL) water

1 tbsp (15 mL) pure maple syrup

1 tsp (5 mL) ground cinnamon

¼ cup (60 mL) almond butter

½ cup (125 mL) Spiced Coconut Granola (page 39) or store-bought

1. Combine the apples and water in a medium frying pan over medium heat. Cover with a lid or baking sheet; cook, stirring occasionally, for about 4 minutes, until softened. Add the maple syrup and cinnamon and stir to coat the apples.

2. Divide the apples between 2 bowls or medium mason jars and add 2 tbsp (30 mL) almond butter to each. Sprinkle ¼ cup (60 mL) granola overtop each. Serve immediately or cover and store in the fridge for up to 1 day. Uncover and microwave on High for 45 seconds to 1 minute before serving, if desired.

Almond Butter Toast with Caramelized Bananas

• SERVES 2 ⱱ TIME: 10 MINUTES •

Avocado toast gets all the love, but I promise you won't be disappointed by this sweet toast. Caramelizing the bananas takes this breakfast delight up a notch, making it feel extra special and fancy with little effort. As an added bonus, the almond butter adds protein and keeps you full longer.

Caramelized Bananas

1 tbsp (15 mL) vegan butter

1 tbsp (15 mL) brown sugar

2 ripe bananas, sliced

¼ tsp (1 mL) ground cinnamon

Toast

4 slices bread, toasted

¼ cup (60 mL) creamy almond butter (approx.)

Pure maple syrup (optional)

Unsweetened large coconut flakes (optional)

Cacao nibs or dairy-free chocolate chips (optional)

1. Melt the vegan butter in a large frying pan over medium heat. Add the brown sugar and stir constantly until dissolved. Add the banana slices and cook for about 5 minutes, stirring occasionally, until golden, sticky and caramelized.

2. Spread about 1 tbsp (15 mL) almond butter on each slice of toast (or more if you like). Evenly divide the caramelized bananas between the slices and sprinkle with maple syrup, coconut and/or cacao nibs (if using).

My Tips

To make this toast nut-free, use your favorite nut-free spread instead of almond butter.

Sometimes I use a vegan chocolate hazelnut spread instead of almond butter, when I want to something more chocolatey for breakfast.

Mini Chocolate Lava Pancakes

These pancakes have the richest, most decadent chocolate flavor, like the breakfast version of a molten lava cake. If I am having people over for brunch, I double the recipe and serve them with fresh berries and coconut whipped cream.

1 cup (250 mL) unbleached all-purpose flour

1 tsp (5 mL) baking powder

2 tbsp (30 mL) organic cane sugar

2 tbsp (30 mL) unsweetened cocoa powder

1 cup (250 mL) unsweetened nondairy milk

1 tsp (5 mL) white vinegar

3 tbsp (45 mL) vegetable oil, divided

Pure maple syrup (optional)

Fresh berries (optional)

Coconut whipped cream (optional)

1. Whisk together the flour, baking powder, cane sugar and cocoa powder in a large bowl until combined.

2. Combine the nondairy milk, vinegar and 1 tbsp (15 mL) oil in a medium bowl. Add to the flour mixture and stir until just combined (a few lumps are okay).

3. Heat a large frying pan over medium heat. Add 1 tbsp (15 mL) oil and spread it around to coat the bottom of the pan. Working in batches, spoon 2 tbsp (30 mL) batter into the pan for each pancake (you should be able to cook 5 pancakes at once). Cook for about 1 minute, until bubbles rise to the surface and burst and the edges look cooked. Flip and cook another 30 seconds to 1 minute, until the batter is set around the edges. Repeat with the remaining oil and batter.

4. Serve with maple syrup, fresh berries and/or coconut whipped cream (if using).

Half-Baked Cookie Dough Pancakes

• MAKES 6 PANCAKES (ABOUT 2 SERVINGS) • ⦿ • TIME: 20 MINUTES •

There is a restaurant in Brooklyn called Champs Diner that serves cookie dough pancakes. Although I haven't been there to try them myself, I have dreamed about them (I will get there some day!). My take on them tastes something like a cross between a pancake and a half-baked cookie. You'll want to break out this recipe from time to time when oatmeal and smoothies just won't cut it.

½ cup (125 mL) Edible Cookie Dough (page 200)

1 cup (250 mL) unbleached all-purpose flour

1½ tsp (7 mL) baking powder

½ tsp (2 mL) ground cinnamon

½ ripe banana, mashed

1¼ cups (300 mL) unsweetened nondairy milk

1½ tsp (7 mL) white vinegar

1 tsp (5 mL) vanilla extract

¼ cup (60 mL) vegetable oil, divided

Organic icing (confectioners') sugar (optional)

Pure maple syrup (optional)

1. Whisk together the flour, baking powder and cinnamon in a large bowl until well combined.

2. Whisk together the mashed banana, nondairy milk, vinegar, vanilla and 2 tbsp (30 mL) oil in a medium bowl. Add the banana mixture to the flour mixture and stir until just combined (a few lumps are okay).

3. Heat a large frying pan over medium heat. Add 1 tbsp (15 mL) oil and spread it around to coat the bottom of the pan. Working in batches, spoon ⅓ cup (75 mL) batter into the pan for each pancake (you should be able to cook 3 pancakes at once). Cook for about 3 minutes, until bubbles rise to the surface and burst and the edges look cooked. Flip and cook for another 30 seconds to 1 minute, until golden brown. Repeat with the remaining oil and batter.

4. Serve each pancake with a spoonful of edible cookie dough on top and a sprinkle of icing sugar and/or a drizzle of maple syrup (if using).

My Tip
This recipe can be doubled
or tripled if you are feeding
more than 2 people (or if you
just really like pancakes!).

Crispy Breakfast Potatoes

• SERVES 2 • • TIME: 30 MINUTES •

I make these breakfast potatoes when I have a bit of time on my hands and feel like making a more elaborate breakfast spread (hint: these are perfect for when you're hosting a brunch). My favorite way to eat these is with Crispy Avocado Open-Face Sandwiches (page 59) or Southwest Scramble Toast (page 63).

6 cups (1.5 L) water

½ lb (250 g) red potatoes, chopped

2 tbsp (30 mL) olive oil

½ tsp (2 mL) salt

¼ tsp (1 mL) freshly ground black pepper

½ tsp (2 mL) paprika

¼ tsp (1 mL) garlic powder

1. Place the water and potatoes in a large pot and bring to a boil over high heat. Reduce the heat to medium-high and cook for about 10 minutes, until the potatoes can be pierced with a fork but aren't falling apart. Drain and set aside.

2. Heat a large frying pan over medium heat. Add the oil, potatoes, salt, pepper, paprika and garlic powder and stir to coat. Cook, stirring frequently, for about 10 minutes, until golden brown. Remove from heat and serve.

My Tips

To take these breakfast potatoes to the next level, try adding other seasonings along with the salt and pepper. Here are some combinations I love:

Spicy Cheese Breakfast Potatoes: ½ tsp (2 mL) chili powder + 1 tbsp (15 mL) nutritional yeast *Extra-Smoky Breakfast Potatoes:* ½ tsp (2 mL) smoked paprika + ½ tsp (2 mL) hot pepper flakes *Garlic Rosemary Breakfast Potatoes:* ½ tsp (2 mL) onion powder + ¼ tsp (1 mL) garlic powder + ¼ tsp (1 mL) dried rosemary.

Breakfast Tea Biscuits

• MAKES 8 BISCUITS • • TIME: 20 MINUTES •

When I was growing up, my mom used to make us tea biscuits regularly. We loved eating them for breakfast, warm out of the oven and slathered with jam.

1½ cups (375 mL) unbleached all-purpose flour (approx.)

2 tsp (10 mL) baking powder

1 tsp (5 mL) organic cane sugar

¼ tsp (1 mL) salt

½ cup (125 mL) unsweetened almond milk or soy milk

2 tsp (10 mL) white vinegar

3 tbsp (45 mL) cold vegan butter

2 tbsp (30 mL) melted vegan butter (optional)

Pastry blender (optional)

Rimmed baking sheet

Thin-edged drinking glass (approx. 3 inches/7.5 cm in diameter), dipped in all-purpose flour

1. Preheat the oven to 425°F (220°C).

2. Whisk together the flour, baking powder, sugar and salt in a large bowl.

3. Combine the almond milk and vinegar in a measuring cup. Set aside.

4. Using two knives or a pastry blender, cut the butter into the flour mixture until crumbly. Add 6 tablespoons (90 mL) almond milk mixture and stir until a dough forms. You want it to be slightly sticky but not too wet. (Depending on the temperature and humidity, you may need more almond milk mixture.) Discard any remaining almond milk mixture.

5. Gently knead the dough in the bowl 3 to 4 times. Transfer to a lightly floured surface. Shape the dough into a disc approximately ½ inch (1 cm) thick. Using a prepared drinking glass, cut the dough into large rounds, twisting the glass slightly when it gets to the bottom. Dip the glass into more flour as needed to prevent sticking.

6. Place the biscuits on the baking sheet in two rows, slightly touching each other.

7. OPTIONAL: For golden brown tops, brush the top of each biscuit with melted butter.

8. Bake in the preheated oven for 10 minutes, until risen and golden brown.

9. Let cool on the pan for 2 minutes. Enjoy warm. Once cooled completely, store in an airtight container at room temperature for up to 2 days or refrigerate for up to 4 days.

My Tip
The biscuits can be frozen and
stored in an airtight container
for up to 1 month. To reheat,
remove from the freezer and
heat in the microwave on
Low in 15-second intervals,
until warm but not hot
(overheating can make
biscuits tough and dry).

Crispy Avocado Open-Face Sandwiches

• SERVES 2 ▽ TIME: 40 MINUTES •

This recipe was inspired by the avocado fries recipe I made on my YouTube channel. Avocado fries are chunks of avocado coated in a crispy batter and baked until golden brown. The outsides are light and crispy while the insides are creamy, almost like a soft cheese. I like them so much I decided to find a way to eat them for breakfast! These open-face sandwiches are piled high with crispy avocado fries, greens, tomato and a savory cashew cream sauce.

Avocado Fries

3 tbsp (45 mL) all-purpose flour

¼ cup (60 mL) unsweetened nondairy milk

1 cup (250 mL) panko bread crumbs

2 tbsp (30 mL) nutritional yeast

¼ tsp (1 mL) onion powder

¼ tsp (1 mL) salt

1 ripe avocado, sliced into thick wedges

Cashew Cream Sauce

1 cup (250 mL) raw cashews

½ cup (125 mL) water

2 tbsp (30 mL) freshly squeezed

lemon juice

2 tbsp (30 mL) nutritional yeast

½ tsp (2 mL) salt

¼ tsp (1 mL) garlic powder

1 tsp (5 mL) Dijon mustard

Sandwiches

2 English muffins, split in half and toasted

1 cup (250 mL) arugula or baby spinach

1 tomato, sliced

Rimmed baking sheet, lined with parchment paper

High-powered blender (see My Tip)

1. **AVOCADO FRIES:** Preheat the oven to 375°F (190°C).

2. Whisk together the flour and nondairy milk in a small bowl, until smooth.

3. Combine the panko, nutritional yeast, onion powder and salt in a medium bowl.

CONTINUED ON PAGE 60

4. Dip one piece of avocado into the milk mixture and submerge until coated. Allow excess liquid to drip off, then gently dip it in the panko mixture until coated. Place on the prepared baking sheet and repeat with the remaining avocado wedges, spacing them apart on the sheet.

5. Bake in the preheated oven for 25 minutes, flipping after 15 minutes, until golden brown.

6. **CASHEW CREAM SAUCE:** Meanwhile, place the cashews, water, lemon juice, nutritional yeast, salt, garlic powder and Dijon mustard in the blender. Blend on high speed for 1 to 2 minutes, until smooth and creamy.

7. Divide the arugula between the English muffin halves, followed by the tomato and avocado fries. Evenly pour the sauce overtop; serve.

My Tip

If you don't have a high-powered blender, soak the cashews in a small bowl with enough hot water to cover for 1 hour prior to blending, then drain and add to the blender. This will soften them up and allow you to achieve a smoother consistency.

Chickpea Scramble

Chickpea scramble is a great alternative to tofu scramble for people who can't or don't eat soy. It is also high in protein and fiber and super tasty. Try it on toast with a side of Crispy Breakfast Potatoes (page 55) or in a pita with greens, vegan cheese and salsa.

1 tbsp (15 mL) nutritional yeast

½ tsp (2 mL) chili powder

¼ tsp (1 mL) ground turmeric

¼ tsp (1 mL) salt

¼ tsp (1 mL) freshly ground black pepper

2 tbsp (30 mL) water

1 can (14 oz/398 mL) chickpeas, drained and rinsed

1 tbsp (15 mL) olive oil

⅓ cup (75 mL) chopped white onion

1 garlic clove, minced

1 cup (250 mL) chopped bell pepper

1. Whisk together the nutritional yeast, chili powder, turmeric, salt, pepper and water in a small bowl.

2. Lightly mash the chickpeas in a medium bowl until they are broken up and resemble the texture of scrambled eggs.

3. Heat a medium frying pan over medium heat. Add the oil, onion and garlic; cook, stirring frequently, for 3 minutes, until softened. Add the bell pepper and cook, stirring frequently, for 2 minutes, until slightly softened.

4. Add the chickpeas to the pan and pour the spice mixture overtop. Cook for 5 minutes, stirring frequently, until the water has evaporated. Serve.

Southwest Scramble Toast

• SERVES 2 ▽ TIME: 15 MINUTES •

There are entire Pinterest boards dedicated to stuff on toast. Having perused said boards for inspiration, I have made it my personal mission to see how much planty goodness I can get on one piece of toast. This smoky and filling version is piled so high with veggies and tofu you may need to use a fork! The turmeric is added for color, so don't worry about leaving it out if you don't have any on hand.

1 tbsp (15 mL) olive oil

¼ cup (60 mL) chopped red onion

½ cup (125 mL) chopped green bell pepper

½ cup (125 mL) chopped red bell pepper

12 oz (375 g) extra-firm tofu, crumbled

1 tbsp (15 mL) nutritional yeast

½ tsp (2 mL) salt

½ tsp (2 mL) chili powder

¼ tsp (1 mL) smoked paprika

¼ tsp (1 mL) garlic powder

¼ tsp (1 mL) ground turmeric (optional)

2 tbsp (30 mL) water

4 slices whole-grain bread, toasted

2 tbsp (30 mL) chopped cilantro (optional)

1. Heat a medium frying pan over medium heat. Add the oil, onion, red pepper and green pepper; cook for 3 minutes, stirring frequently, until softened. Add the tofu and cook for another 3 minutes, until slightly browned.

2. Meanwhile, whisk together the nutritional yeast, salt, chili powder, paprika, garlic powder, turmeric (if using) and water until well combined. Pour over the scramble and stir to coat. Cook for another 3 minutes, stirring frequently, until fragrant and browned.

3. Evenly divide the scramble and pile on top of the pieces of toast. Sprinkle the cilantro overtop (if using). Serve.

My Tip

This scramble can also be turned into a delicious breakfast burrito. Swap out the toast for a tortilla and fill it with vegan cheese, salsa and vegan sour cream.

Savory Breakfast Bowls

• SERVES 2 ⱴ TIME: 25 MINUTES •

I love savory breakfasts, and this bowl is perfect for weekday meal prep. It's also super easy to double so that you can have prepared breakfasts in the fridge. Make sure to keep the sauce separate until serving and wait until then to cut the avocado.

Breakfast Bowls

Water

1 cup (250 mL) quinoa, rinsed

1 large sweet potato, peeled and cut into small cubes

2 tbsp (30 mL) olive oil

1 cup (250 mL) sliced button mushrooms

¼ cup (60 mL) chopped green onion

¼ tsp (1 mL) salt

¼ tsp (1 mL) pepper

Tahini Sauce

¼ cup (60 mL) tahini

3 tbsp (45 mL) warm water

1 tbsp (15 mL) freshly squeezed lemon juice

1 tbsp (15 mL) nutritional yeast

2 tsp (10 mL) pure maple syrup or brown sugar

1 tsp (5 mL) reduced-sodium soy sauce

1 garlic clove, finely minced

Extra Toppings

1 cup (250 mL) cherry tomatoes, halved

1 ripe avocado, sliced (optional)

1. **BREAKFAST BOWLS:** Cook the quinoa according to the package directions. Set aside.

2. Meanwhile, fill a medium pot with 2 inches (5 cm) water and bring it to a boil over high heat. Fit a steamer basket over the top and place the sweet potato inside. Cover and steam for about 5 minutes, until easily pierced with a fork.

3. Heat a frying pan over medium heat. Add the oil, cooked sweet potato, mushrooms, green onion, salt and pepper; cook for about 5 minutes, stirring frequently, until the mushrooms are softened and starting to brown. Set aside.

4. **TAHINI SAUCE:** Whisk together the tahini, warm water, lemon juice, nutritional yeast, maple syrup, soy sauce and garlic in a small bowl.

5. Divide the quinoa and the sweet potato mixture between 2 bowls. Evenly divide the cherry tomatoes and avocado (if using) between each and drizzle the sauce overtop.

My Tip

This bowl can be customized in many different ways. For a higher-protein version, add ½ cup (125 mL) cubed firm tofu to the frying pan with the mushrooms. If you want to add some green to your bowl, throw in a handful of fresh baby spinach or alfalfa sprouts just before serving.

Snacks &
Small Bites

My Tip

Let the cooked tofu cool completely on the baking sheet. Place in a resealable freezer bag or airtight container and store in the freezer for up to 3 months. To reheat, simply bake from frozen for 10 minutes in an oven preheated to 400°F (200°C), flipping the pieces halfway through.

Crispy Tofu Dippers

• SERVES 4 ♡ TIME: 35 MINUTES •

These tofu dippers are the perfect high-protein snack and great to serve with a variety of dips. I love them with Vegan "Honey Mustard" Dip (page 17), ketchup or Spicy Lime Mayo (page 18). They freeze really well (see My Tip), so I often make a batch to put straight into the freezer. I use whole wheat bread crumbs for the coating because that gives them the best color, but feel free to use whatever crumbs you like.

12 oz (375 g) firm tofu

½ cup (125 mL) all-purpose flour

½ tsp (2 mL) salt

½ tsp (2 mL) black pepper

1 cup (250 mL) dry whole wheat or panko bread crumbs

½ cup (125 mL) nutritional yeast

½ cup (125 mL) unsweetened nondairy milk

Rimmed baking sheet, lined with parchment paper

1. Preheat the oven to 400°F (200°C).

2. Press the tofu to remove excess moisture (see page 4 for more information).

3. Cut the tofu into ½-inch (1 cm) slices, then cut those diagonally into triangles. Set aside.

4. Whisk together the flour, salt and pepper in a medium bowl.

5. Place the bread crumbs and nutritional yeast in a shallow dish; stir to combine.

6. Pour the nondairy milk into a shallow dish.

7. Dip a piece of tofu in the flour mixture, ensuring that all sides are coated. Dip it in the nondairy milk and then immediately into the breadcrumb mixture, pressing to ensure that all sides are coated in crumbs. Place on the prepared baking sheet and repeat with the remaining tofu, spacing the pieces apart.

8. Bake in the preheated oven for 10 minutes, then flip. Bake for another 10 minutes, until crispy and golden brown.

9. Serve immediately with your favorite dipping sauce or prepare for freezing (see My Tip).

Avocado Fried Toast

There is a running joke that millennials don't buy houses because we spend too much money on avocado toast. If you have ever seen avocado toast on a menu at a restaurant you know it is VERY pricey. That's why I like making my own restaurant-worthy version at home and take it up a notch by frying the bread first. Frying bread is like making a grilled cheese sandwich without the cheese. It gets warm and super crispy and you can then top it with mashed avocado for a DIY version that won't break the bank.

2 tbsp (30 mL) extra virgin olive oil

2 slices whole-grain bread

1 ripe avocado, mashed

2 tsp (10 mL) nutritional yeast

Salt and freshly ground black pepper

Hot pepper flakes (optional)

1. Heat a large frying pan over medium heat. Add the oil and tilt the pan to distribute evenly. Add the bread slices in a single layer. Cook for 2 to 3 minutes per side or until golden and crispy.

2. Remove the bread from the pan and spread half of the mashed avocado on each slice. Sprinkle each slice with 1 tsp (5 mL) nutritional yeast. Add salt, pepper and hot pepper flakes to taste (if using). Serve.

Sweet and Salty Popcorn

• SERVES 4 • • TIME: 5 MINUTES •

I have a popular video series on my YouTube channel called "movie night snacks." I've made cake pops, cheesy pull-apart bread and Buffalo chickpea pizza, but I realized I had forgotten the classic sweet and salty popcorn and knew I wanted it to be in my book. This recipe is super easy and tastes like the more expensive kettle-corn brands you can buy at the grocery store.

3 tbsp (45 mL) vegan butter

2 tbsp (30 mL) pure maple syrup

¼ tsp (1 mL) sea salt

8 cups (2 L) plain, unsalted popped popcorn (see My Tips)

1. Combine the vegan butter, maple syrup and sea salt in a small bowl. Microwave on High for 15 to 20 seconds, until the butter is melted. Stir to combine.

2. Place the popped popcorn in a large bowl. Drizzle the butter mixture overtop and toss to coat. (You may need to do it in 2 batches to ensure that all the popcorn gets coated.) Serve.

My Tips

For 8 cups of popped popcorn, start with about ¼ cup (60 mL) kernels.

For a salted chocolate flavor, add 1 tsp (5 mL) cocoa powder to the melted butter mixture.

Cheesy Warm Nachos

• SERVES 4 • • TIME: 20 MINUTES •

Nachos are among my favorite shareable foods. One of the best things about this recipe is that anytime I make it, even my non-vegan friends go crazy for the flavor. I always bake them to give the cheese sauce a chance to heat up and get super gooey — it reminds me of the nacho cheese served at carnivals and movie theaters.

1 bag (10 oz/295 g) tortilla chips

1 recipe Cheese Sauce (page 19) or 1½ cups (375 mL) vegan cheese shreds

1 can (14 oz/398 mL) vegan refried beans

1 green bell pepper, thinly sliced

1 red bell pepper, thinly sliced

½ cup (125 mL) finely chopped red onion

1 jalapeño pepper, seeded and sliced

Chopped fresh cilantro (optional)

1 recipe Five-Minute Guacamole (page 78) or 1½ cups (375 mL) store-bought

1 cup (250 mL) store-bought or homemade tomato salsa

Vegan sour cream (optional)

Rimmed baking sheet

1. Preheat the oven to 375°F (190°C).

2. Spread the tortilla chips in a single layer on the baking sheet. Drizzle half the cheese sauce or ¾ cup (175 mL) cheese shreds overtop. Dollop the refried beans over the nachos. Sprinkle the green pepper, red pepper and onion overtop in an even layer. Add the remaining cheese sauce or shreds, then bake in the preheated oven for about 10 minutes, until the cheese is hot and bubbling slightly. Make sure to keep an eye on the nachos so the chips don't burn.

3. Remove from the oven and serve hot, sprinkled with cilantro (if using). Serve with the guacamole, salsa and vegan sour cream (if using) alongside for dipping.

My Tip

Vegan refried beans are pretty easy to find, but I have seen some that include lard. Always make sure to read the label before purchasing.

Maple Cinnamon Pecans

• MAKES 1¼ CUPS (300 ML) • • TIME: 8 MINUTES •

These pecans are amazing for a snack or as a topping for oatmeal or salads such as my Strawberry Spinach Salad with Buttermilk-Style Dressing (page 135). A lot of sweetened roasted nut recipes require a long baking time, but this one can be made in under 10 minutes on the stove, so you can easily pull these out of your hat whenever the craving hits.

1 tbsp (15 mL) pure maple syrup

1 tbsp (15 mL) brown sugar

¼ tsp (1 mL) ground cinnamon

2 tsp (10 mL) vegan butter

1¼ cups (300 mL) pecan halves

⅛ tsp (0.5 mL) salt

Rimmed baking sheet, lined with parchment paper

1. Combine the maple syrup, brown sugar and cinnamon in a small bowl; whisk until smooth.

2. Heat a medium frying pan over medium heat. Add the vegan butter and heat until melted, tilting the pan to distribute evenly. Add the pecans and cook for 2 minutes, occasionally stirring gently, until lightly toasted.

3. Add the maple syrup mixture to the pan and stir continuously for about 1 minute, until the pecans are coated.

4. Spread the pecans in a single layer on the prepared baking sheet. Sprinkle with the salt and let cool completely. Serve or store in an airtight container in a cool, dry place for up to 2 weeks.

Spicy Mango Salsa

• MAKES APPROX. 3 CUPS (750 ML) • 🌿 👤 • TIME: 10 MINUTES •

This is a great recipe for parties, whether you are hosting or attending. And you can make it the day before to save time — it tastes even better after it's had some time to sit.

1½ cups (375 mL) diced fresh mango

1 cup (250 mL) diced tomatoes

1 red bell pepper, finely chopped

1 jalapeño pepper, seeded and minced

⅓ cup (75 mL) finely chopped red onion

¼ cup (60 mL) freshly squeezed lime juice

¼ cup (60 mL) finely chopped fresh cilantro (optional)

1. Combine the mango, tomatoes, bell pepper, jalapeño, onion, lime juice and cilantro (if using) in a medium bowl. Serve immediately or transfer to an airtight container and store in the fridge for up to 3 days.

Five-Minute Guacamole

• MAKES 1½ CUPS (375 ML) • 🌿 👤 • TIME: 5 MINUTES •

What's better than guacamole? Guacamole that takes only five minutes to make!

2 large ripe avocados, halved

2 tbsp (30 mL) freshly squeezed lime juice

¼ tsp (1 mL) salt

¼ tsp (1 mL) freshly ground pepper

1. Scoop the avocado into a medium bowl. Mash with a fork until mostly smooth, with a few lumps remaining. Add the lime juice, salt and pepper; stir to combine. Serve.

My Tip

Give the guac some extra oomph by adding ¼ cup (60 mL) minced red onion and ½ cup (125 mL) diced fresh tomato for a chunky, flavorful dip.

Chocolate Chia Pudding

• SERVES 4 • • TIME: 10 MINUTES (PLUS 6 HOURS FOR SOAKING) •

I ate a lot of chocolate pudding when I was young. When I got older and discovered chia seeds — and subsequently chia pudding — I was pleasantly surprised to find that the taste and texture of blended chocolate chia pudding very closely resembles the pudding I used to eat regularly. Now I like to take it a step further and add a mountain of toppings such as fresh berries and a dollop of coconut whipped cream.

1⅓ cups (325 mL) unsweetened nondairy milk

¼ cup (60 mL) chia seeds

¼ cup (60 mL) unsweetened cocoa powder

¼ cup (60 mL) pure maple syrup

¼ tsp (1 mL) vanilla extract

Optional Toppings

Fresh berries

Vegan chocolate chips

Coconut whipped cream

Blender

1. Combine the nondairy milk, chia seeds, cocoa powder, maple syrup and vanilla in an airtight container; whisk to combine. Cover with the lid and refrigerate for at least 6 hours or up to overnight.

2. Transfer to the blender and blend on high speed for 1 to 2 minutes, until smooth (see My Tip).

3. Pour into 4 bowls to serve immediately or store in an airtight container in the fridge for up to 3 days. Top with berries, chocolate chips and/or coconut whipped cream, if desired.

> **My Tip**
> If you enjoy the thick and slightly crunchy texture of unblended chia pudding, feel free to skip the blending step. However, I know that many people (like me) prefer a smooth pudding, so I like to blend it until it's smooth and creamy.

Vegan Snackboard with Easy Spreadable Cheese

• MAKES 1¼ CUPS (300 ML) CHEESE • • TIME: 20 MINUTES (PLUS 1 HOUR FOR SOAKING) •

This spreadable cheese is amazing for cheese boards. For dinner parties I love creating beautiful spreads with fruit, veggies, crackers, homemade cheeses and vegan meats. (I even made a video about it that became super popular over the holidays — for good reason!) Here I give you my favorite basic spreadable cheese recipe and some ideas for assembling a snackboard for your next party.

Easy Spreadable Vegan Cheese

1½ cups (375 mL) raw cashews

3 tbsp (45 mL) water (approx.)

2 tbsp (30 mL) olive oil

2 tbsp (30 mL) freshly squeezed lemon juice

¼ cup (60 mL) nutritional yeast

¼ tsp (1 mL) garlic powder

¼ tsp (1 mL) salt

¼ tsp (1 mL) pepper

Snackboard Options

Berries (strawberries and blueberries work really well)

Figs

Crackers

Vegan chocolate

Almonds

Walnuts

Cherry tomatoes

Sliced cucumber

Sliced carrots

Sliced bell pepper

Food processor or high-powered blender

1. **EASY SPREADABLE VEGAN CHEESE:** Soak the cashews for 1 hour in enough hot water to cover. Drain and discard the water.

2. Place the soaked cashews, water, oil, lemon juice, nutritional yeast, garlic powder, salt and pepper in the food processor. Process for 4 to 5 minutes, scraping down the sides of the bowl as needed, until smooth and thick.

3. Transfer the cheese to a serving bowl. Assemble your snackboard using the optional ingredients. Serve with the cheese.

My Tip

You can make the cheese ahead of time and store it in an airtight container in the fridge for up to 4 days.

Sun-Dried Tomato and Spinach Pinwheels

• MAKES 10 PINWHEELS • • TIME: 20 MINUTES •

These pinwheels are the ultimate finger food for a party — or to hoard all for yourself as a snack. They're creamy and cheesy but also fresh, thanks to the spinach. While the oven is preheating, combine the filling ingredients, spread the filling on the puff pastry, roll it up, slice and bake. It doesn't get much easier than that!

Filling

½ cup (125 mL) vegan cream cheese

½ cup (125 mL) drained and chopped oil-packed sun-dried tomatoes

¼ tsp (1 mL) garlic powder

½ tsp (2 mL) dried basil

¼ cup (60 mL) vegan Parmesan cheese

½ cup (125 mL) chopped baby spinach

Pastry

1 sheet (8½ by 12 inches/22 by 30 cm) vegan puff pastry

Rimmed baking sheet, lined with parchment paper

1. Preheat the oven to 375°F (190°C).

2. **FILLING:** Combine the vegan cream cheese, sun-dried tomatoes, garlic powder, basil, vegan Parmesan and spinach in a mixing bowl.

3. **PASTRY:** Lay the puff pastry sheet on a work surface with a long side facing you. Spread the cheese mixture over the pastry in an even layer. Starting from the edge closest to you, roll the pastry into a cylinder, tucking it over the filling as you go. Cut into 10 slices approximately 1-1/4 inches (3 cm) thick. Lay the slices flat on the prepared baking sheet, spacing 2 inches (5 cm) apart.

4. Bake in the preheated oven for 12 minutes, or until golden brown and puffed up. Remove from the oven and let cool on the pan for 5 minutes before serving.

My Tip

The filling can be prepared up to a day in advance and kept in an airtight container in the fridge until ready to use. Assemble and bake the pinwheels shortly before serving.

Chocolate-Dipped Fruit Pops

• MAKES 10 PIECES • • TIME: 15 MINUTES (PLUS 30 MINUTES FOR CHILLING) •

Dipping fruit in chocolate has become a full-blown obsession. It started with strawberries, but now there aren't many fruits I wouldn't enjoy with a thick coating of chocolate. I make these fruit pops when I have the girls over for wine and snacks. They are the perfect fuss-free sweet treat to share with friends.

¾ cup (175 mL) vegan chocolate chips

1 tsp (5 mL) coconut oil

1 banana, halved lengthwise

1 plum, pit removed, quartered

4 cherries or strawberries, stems left on

Optional Toppings

Vegan sprinkles

Crushed pistachio nuts

Chia seeds

Coconut shreds

Sea salt

Rimmed baking sheet, lined with parchment paper

6 wooden skewers

1. Combine the vegan chocolate chips and coconut oil in a heatproof glass or ceramic bowl. Microwave on High for 20 to 30 seconds, until softened; stir. Heat in 20-second intervals, stirring between each, until the chocolate is melted and smooth. Do not overheat; stirring usually helps to melt the chocolate, and that way you can avoid burning it.

2. Insert skewers into the banana halves and plum quarters. Dip halfway into the chocolate, then let the excess drip off before laying them on the prepared baking sheet. Sprinkle immediately with optional toppings. Hold the cherries and strawberries by their stems and repeat the dipping process. Sprinkle immediately with optional toppings.

3. Refrigerate the fruit for at least 30 minutes, until the chocolate hardens, or for up to 6 hours. Serve.

Chocolate Chip Banana Bread in a Mug

Sometimes I really want a bit of banana bread just for me and don't want to take time to make an entire loaf. That's how microwavable banana bread in a mug was born. I love that in just five minutes you can have a sweet treat that uses only one dish.

¼ cup (60 mL) all-purpose flour

2 tbsp (30 mL) organic cane sugar

¼ tsp (1 mL) baking powder

1 tbsp (15 mL) vegetable oil

½ medium ripe banana, mashed

3 tbsp (45 mL) unsweetened nondairy milk

1 tbsp (15 mL) vegan chocolate chips

1. Combine the flour, sugar and baking powder in a large mug; stir until smooth. Add the oil, mashed banana, nondairy milk and chocolate chips; stir until combined, scraping the bottom of the mug to incorporate all the dry ingredients.

2. Microwave on High for 1½ minutes or until a tester inserted in the center comes out clean.

My Tip

Don't let appearances deceive you when you're making this recipe. The center cooks first in a microwave, while the top may appear slightly undercooked. Make sure to check with a tester so you don't under- or overcook the banana bread. You may need to adjust the cooking time, depending on the wattage of your microwave.

Snickerdoodle Mug Cake

• SERVES 1 ♡ TIME: 5 MINUTES •

Mug cakes make a regular appearance on my YouTube channel — my most popular recipe, a chocolate mug cake, has over two million views! When I want to mix things up, I make one that is snickerdoodle-flavored. For the uninitiated, that's a cake version of a cinnamon-sugar butter cookie. Mine is vegan, of course.

¼ cup (60 mL) all-purpose flour

3 tbsp (45 mL) organic cane sugar

½ tsp (2 mL) ground cinnamon

¼ tsp (1 mL) baking powder

¼ cup (60 mL) unsweetened nondairy milk

2 tbsp (30 mL) vegetable oil

¼ tsp (1 mL) vanilla extract

Vegan vanilla ice cream or coconut whipped cream (optional)

1. Combine the flour, sugar, cinnamon and baking soda in a mug. Add the nondairy milk, oil and vanilla; stir until just combined, scraping the bottom of the mug to incorporate all the dry ingredients.

2. Microwave on High for 1 minute and 15 seconds, or until a tester inserted in the center comes out clean. Remove from the microwave and let cool for 1 minute.

3. Serve with a spoonful of a vegan vanilla ice cream or coconut whipped cream, if desired.

My Tip

Don't let appearances deceive you when you're making this recipe. The center cooks first in a microwave, while the top may appear slightly undercooked. Make sure to check with a tester so you don't under- or overcook the mug cake. You may need to adjust the cooking time, depending on the wattage of your microwave.

Soups & Sides

Famous Lasagna Soup

• SERVES 4 ♥ TIME: 40 MINUTES •

Two years ago I made a video on my YouTube channel called "Vegan Recipes for Lazy Days," which included this recipe. The video was a huge hit and people all over the world discovered the wonder that is this soup. It tastes like lasagna but requires only one pot and 30 minutes to make. It's basically magic.

1 tbsp (15 mL) olive oil

½ onion, finely chopped

1 bell pepper, chopped

1 cup (250 mL) finely chopped mushrooms

2½ cups (625 mL) Marinara Sauce (page 12) or store-bought

3½ cups (875 mL) vegetable broth

½ cup (125 mL) dried brown lentils

8 lasagna noodles, broken into pieces

1 cup (250 mL) baby spinach

1 batch Vegan Ricotta (page 20) or ½ cup (125 mL) vegan cheese shreds

Chopped fresh flat-leaf (Italian) parsley (optional)

Freshly ground black pepper (optional)

1. Heat a large pot over medium heat. Add the oil, onion, bell pepper and mushrooms; cook for about 5 minutes, stirring frequently, until the onion is translucent.

2. Add the marinara sauce, vegetable broth, lentils and lasagna noodles; stir to combine. Reduce the heat and simmer for about 25 minutes, stirring frequently, until the lentils and noodles are tender.

3. Add the spinach and stir to combine. Ladle into 4 bowls and top each with a spoonful of ricotta or vegan cheese shreds. Garnish with fresh parsley and freshly ground black pepper, if desired.

My Tip
Be sure to read the ingredients
list on your curry paste, as
some brands contain seafood.

Takeout Thai Curry Coconut Soup

• SERVES 4 • • TIME: 30 MINUTES •

Making takeout recipes at home is something I love doing on my YouTube channel. They are super popular because it's an easy way to save money and eat a little bit healthier. Thai is on my regular rotation and this recipe was inspired by yellow curry, which I always order.

2 tbsp (30 mL) coconut oil

2 garlic cloves, minced

½ cup (125 mL) chopped green onions

1 cup (250 mL) chopped red bell pepper

1 cup (250 mL) chopped broccoli

1 medium carrot, chopped

3 tbsp (45 mL) Thai yellow curry paste (see My Tip)

½ tsp (2 mL) ground ginger

2 cups (500 mL) vegetable broth

1 cup (250 mL) water

1 can (14 oz/398 mL) full-fat coconut milk

3 tbsp (45 mL) brown sugar

4 oz (125 g) rice vermicelli noodles

1. Heat a medium pot over medium heat. Add the coconut oil and heat until shimmering. Add the garlic and green onions and cook for 3 minutes, stirring frequently, until the garlic is just beginning to brown. Add the bell pepper, broccoli and carrot; cook for 3 to 4 minutes, stirring occasionally, until softened slightly.

2. Add the curry paste, ginger, vegetable broth, water, coconut milk and brown sugar; stir until combined and the curry paste is completely dissolved. Reduce the heat to low and simmer for 10 minutes, stirring occasionally, until the soup has thickened slightly.

3. Meanwhile, cook the noodles in a separate medium pot according to the package directions. Drain.

4. Add the noodles to the curry mixture and stir to combine. Divide evenly among 4 bowls. Serve.

Cheesy Vegetable Soup

• SERVES 4 • • TIME: 30 MINUTES •

This soup is creamy and comforting but still healthy, because it is packed with veggies. I like to serve it with Cheesy Toasted Garlic Bread (page 117), or I sometimes add homemade croutons, like the ones from my Caesar Salad (page 148), to give it a nice crunch.

2 tbsp (30 mL) olive oil

1 onion, about 3 inches (7.5 cm) in diameter, chopped

1 small cauliflower head, chopped into florets

1 medium white potato, peeled and chopped

2 carrots, chopped

4 cups (1 L) no-salt-added vegetable broth

3 tbsp (45 mL) nutritional yeast

1 tsp (5 mL) apple cider vinegar

1 tsp (5 mL) salt

½ tsp (2 mL) garlic powder

½ tsp (2 mL) black pepper

Blender or immersion blender

1. Heat a large pot over medium heat. Add the oil and onion; cook for 5 minutes, stirring frequently, until the onion is translucent.

2. Add the cauliflower, potato, carrot and vegetable broth. Bring to a boil over high heat, then immediately reduce the heat to medium-low and simmer for 10 to 15 minutes, until the vegetables are soft.

3. Add the nutritional yeast, apple cider vinegar, salt, garlic powder and pepper; stir to combine. Let cool slightly.

4. Working in batches, transfer the soup to the blender; blend on high speed for about 1 minute, until smooth. (You can also use an immersion blender to purée the soup in the pot.)

5. Transfer the soup back to pot (if necessary) and heat on medium-low for 5 minutes, stirring occasionally, until warmed through. Divide evenly among 4 bowls. Serve.

Roasted Butternut Squash Soup

· SERVES 4 · · TIME: 1 HOUR 15 MINUTES ·

This super soup contains no dairy (of course) but gets its creaminess from coconut milk. Don't worry if you don't love coconut; you can barely taste it among all the other flavors. This recipe is great to serve alongside Gooey Grilled Cheese Sandwiches (page 130) or a hearty salad like my Simple Apple and Kale Salad (page 144).

1 butternut squash (about 1½ lbs/ 750 g), halved lengthwise and seeded

4 tsp (20 mL) olive oil, divided

½ medium onion, chopped

2 garlic cloves, minced

2 cups (500 mL) low-sodium vegetable broth

1 cup (250 mL) full-fat coconut milk

1 tbsp (15 mL) pure maple syrup

½ tsp (2 mL) salt

¼ tsp (1 mL) black pepper

Additional coconut milk (optional)

Chopped fresh flat-leaf (Italian) parsley (optional)

Rimmed baking sheet, lined with parchment paper

Blender

1. Preheat the oven to 425°F (220°C).

2. Drizzle the cut sides of the squash with 2 tsp (10 mL) oil, then place cut side down on the prepared baking sheet. Bake in the preheated oven for 45 minutes or until fork-tender. Remove from the oven and let cool slightly.

3. Heat a large pot over medium heat. Add the remaining 2 tsp (10 mL) oil, onion and garlic. Cook for 5 minutes, stirring frequently, until the onion is translucent. Remove from the heat.

4. Working in batches as necessary, scoop the cooked squash out of the skin and place in the blender with the vegetable broth, onion and garlic. Blend until smooth and creamy.

5. Transfer the blended squash back into the pot. Add the coconut milk, maple syrup, salt and pepper. Simmer over low heat for 10 minutes, stirring occasionally, until the flavors have melded. Divide evenly among 4 bowls; drizzle with coconut milk and/or top with parsley (if using). Serve.

Cream of Mushroom Soup

• SERVES 4 ♡ TIME: 50 MINUTES •

Mushrooms are really such *fun guys* (fungi, get it?). I love eating this creamy soup with crunchy Cheesy Toasted Garlic Bread (page 117) on the side to soak up all the mushroom-y goodness. When I make a whole recipe for myself, I always have leftovers. Instead of eating it as a soup for multiple days in a row, I sometimes use it in place of pasta sauce or mix it into rice. It may seem odd to use soup as a pasta sauce, but trust me, it tastes great!

¼ cup (60 mL) vegan butter, divided

½ medium onion, chopped

2 garlic cloves, minced

1 lb (500 g) cremini mushrooms, finely chopped

1 lb (500 g) white mushrooms, finely chopped

3 tbsp (45 mL) all-purpose flour

2 cups (500 mL) low-sodium vegetable broth or mushroom broth

1 can (14 oz/398 mL) full-fat coconut milk

1 tsp (5 mL) dried thyme

1 tsp (5 mL) dried parsley

½ tsp (2 mL) salt

¼ tsp (1 mL) black pepper

Blender

1. Heat a large pot over medium heat. Add 1 tbsp (15 mL) vegan butter and heat until melted and simmering. Add the onion and garlic; cook for 5 minutes, stirring frequently, until the onion is translucent. Add the cremini mushrooms and white mushrooms; cook for about 8 minutes, stirring frequently, until they shrink and start to brown.

2. Meanwhile, heat a medium pot over medium heat. Add the remaining 3 tbsp (45 mL) vegan butter and heat until melted and bubbling slightly. Add the flour and stir until a thick paste forms. Slowly add the vegetable broth, ¼ cup (60 mL) at a time, stirring constantly until smooth and thick.

3. Add the broth mixture to the mushroom mixture and stir to combine. Add the coconut milk, thyme, parsley, salt and pepper; stir to combine. Gently simmer for 10 minutes, until thickened slightly. Let cool slightly.

4. Transfer three-quarters of the soup to the blender. Blend on low speed until almost smooth, with just a few chunks remaining.

5. Transfer the soup back into the large pot; heat over medium-low heat for 5 minutes, stirring frequently, until warmed through. Divide evenly among 4 bowls. Serve.

My Tip

This soup can be stored in an airtight container in the fridge for up to 3 days. To reheat, place in a large pot over medium heat and stir frequently for about 5 minutes, or until heated through.

Sesame Mixed Vegetables

• SERVES 4 • • TIME: 15 MINUTES •

This recipe makes a great side dish alongside Vegetable Fried Rice (page 178) or Sweet Chili Tofu and Rice Bowls (page 174). The four-ingredient sesame sauce adds a nice twist to an otherwise "boring" side dish of steamed vegetables. For a super-speedy dinner, serve the vegetables over some cooked quinoa and make a double batch of sauce for drizzling overtop.

1 cup (250 mL) chopped broccoli florets

1 cup (250 mL) chopped cauliflower florets

1 cup (250 mL) baby carrots

1 cup (250 mL) green beans, trimmed

1 garlic clove, minced

1 tbsp (15 mL) soy sauce

2 tsp (10 mL) sesame oil

1½ tbsp (22 mL) pure maple syrup or agave nectar

2 tsp (10 mL) sesame seeds

Hot pepper flakes (optional)

Steamer basket

1. Fill a large pot with 2 inches (5 cm) of water. Cover and bring to a boil over high heat. Fit a steamer basket over the top and place the broccoli, cauliflower and baby carrots inside. Steam for about 4 minutes, until fork-tender. Add the green beans and steam for another 3 minutes, until brightly colored and fork-tender.

2. Combine the garlic, soy sauce, sesame oil and maple syrup in a small bowl. Remove the vegetables from the steamer and place in a serving bowl. Pour the sauce over the vegetables and gently toss to coat. Garnish with sesame seeds and hot pepper flakes (if using). Serve immediately.

Thai Coconut Rice

Coconut rice is a staple at most Thai restaurants, and it is easy to see why. It's so creamy and sweet and pairs amazingly well with spicy vegetable curries. I finally decided to make it at home and was surprised by how easy it was to master. Try this with Sweet Chili Tofu and Rice Bowls (page 174) and Sesame Mixed Vegetables (page 106).

1½ cups (375 mL) short-grain white rice

1 can (14 oz/398 mL) full-fat or light coconut milk

1¼ cups (300 mL) water

½ tsp (2 mL) organic cane sugar

½ tsp (2 mL) salt

1. Rinse the rice in a mesh strainer until the water runs clear.

2. Combine the rice, coconut milk, water, sugar and salt in a medium pot. Bring to a boil over high heat, then immediately reduce the heat to low. Once the liquid has reached a very low simmer, cover with the lid and cook for about 15 to 20 minutes, until all the liquid has been absorbed. Fluff with a fork and serve.

My Tip

Using full-fat coconut milk will result in a creamier consistency and more coconut flavor. However, if you are not a huge fan of coconut, I suggest using light coconut milk, since it will be less coconut-y but will add a nice buttery consistency to the rice.

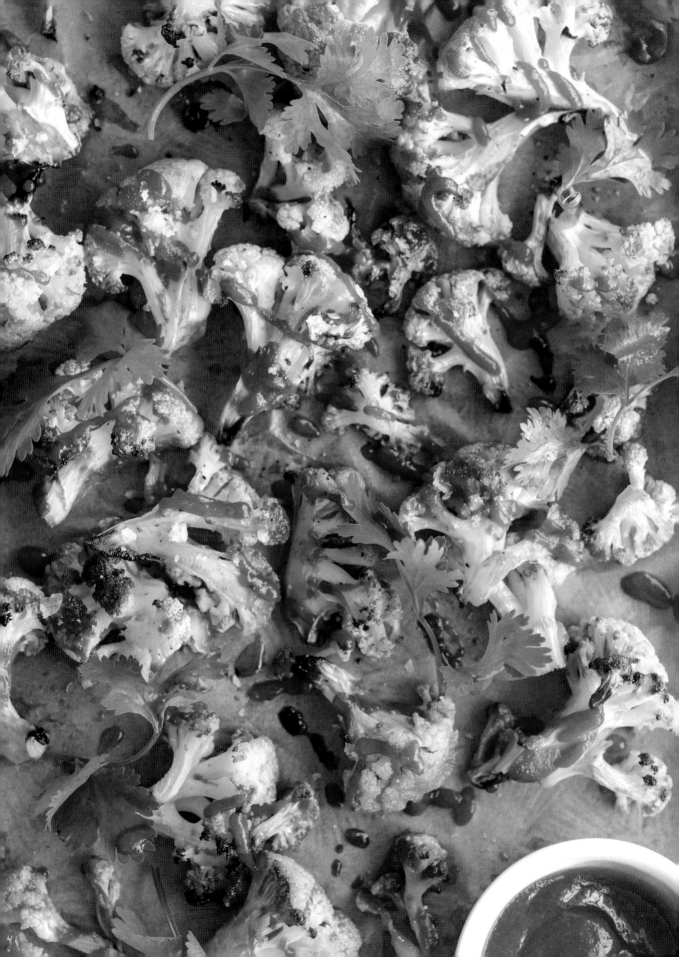

Sweet Sriracha Roasted Cauliflower

• SERVES 4 • • TIME: 30 MINUTES •

This cauliflower recipe makes a nice change from typical roasted veg because of its unique sweet and hot flavors. It makes a great side dish with Chickpea, Lentil and Sweet Potato Curry (page 165), and I also use it in Sweet Sriracha Cauliflower Wraps (page 131).

1 large cauliflower head, chopped into florets

1 tbsp (15 mL) vegetable oil

2 tbsp (30 mL) Sriracha sauce

¼ cup (60 mL) pure maple syrup or agave nectar

¼ tsp (1 mL) salt

Rimmed baking sheet, lined with parchment paper or foil

1. Preheat the oven to 425°F (220°C).

2. Combine the cauliflower and oil in a large bowl; toss to coat.

3. Spread out the cauliflower in an even layer on the prepared baking sheet, setting aside the bowl. Bake in the preheated oven for 10 minutes, until the cauliflower begins to brown.

4. Meanwhile, whisk together the Sriracha sauce and maple syrup in the large bowl.

5. Remove the cauliflower from the oven and return it to the bowl with the Sriracha sauce mixture, setting aside the baking sheet. Toss to coat.

6. Return the cauliflower to the baking sheet, spreading it out in an even layer; sprinkle with the salt and bake for another 15 minutes, until tender. Remove from the oven; serve.

My Tip

Store the roasted cauliflower in an airtight container in the fridge for up to 3 days. To reheat, bake for 15 minutes in an oven preheated to 350°F (180°C), or heat in the microwave for 1 minute or until heated through.

Ginger-Glazed Carrots

• SERVES 4 •   • TIME: 15 MINUTES •

These carrots are an excellent side dish for holiday meals. I serve them with Super-Fluffy Mashed Potatoes (page 120), Crispy Tofu Dippers (page 69) or Sliceable Seitan (page 25) and Veggie Gravy (page 13).

4 large carrots, cut into ¼-inch (0.5 cm) slices

2 tsp (10 mL) vegan butter, melted

1 tsp (5 mL) brown sugar

½ tsp (2 mL) ground ginger

Chopped fresh flat-leaf (Italian) parsley (optional)

Salt

1. Place the carrots in a medium pot and add enough water to cover. Boil over high heat for about 10 minutes or until fork-tender. Drain and set aside.

2. Place the melted vegan butter in a medium serving dish. Add the brown sugar and ginger; stir to combine. Add the cooked carrots and toss to coat. Season with salt to taste and garnish with chopped parsley (if using). Serve.

Broccoli with Cheese Sauce

• SERVES 4 • • TIME: 15 MINUTES •

I don't think this is unusual, but when I was growing up, the only way my parents could get my sister and me to eat broccoli was by serving it with melted Cheddar cheese on top. It's clearly a winning combo, so of course I had to recreate it vegan-style!

4 cups (1 L) broccoli florets

1 recipe Cheese Sauce (page 19) or 2 cups (500 mL) store-bought vegan cheese sauce, warmed

Salt and freshly ground black pepper

Steamer basket

1. Fill a large pot with 2 inches (5 cm) of water and bring to a boil over high heat. Fit a steamer basket over the top, add the broccoli and steam for about 5 minutes, until brightly colored and fork-tender.

2. Transfer the cooked broccoli to a large bowl and drizzle the cheese sauce overtop. Season with salt and pepper to taste.

My Tip
You can substitute 4 cups (1 L) cauliflower florets for the broccoli in this recipe.

Perfectly Photogenic Roasted Veggies

• SERVES 4 • • TIME: 45 MINUTES •

While I don't love the stereotype that vegans only eat vegetables, I must say I do love a good pan of roasted veggies from time to time. A combination of different veggies provides the most beautiful array of colors — you can bet someone will whip out their phone to snap a few photos for Instagram. Who knew plants could be so photogenic? (Actually, I knew! Follow me on Instagram @itslivb wink.)

1 large sweet potato, peeled and chopped

1½ cups (375 mL) halved Brussels sprouts

3 large carrots, peeled and chopped

1 large white potato, peeled and chopped

2 tbsp (30 mL) olive oil

1 tsp (5 mL) salt

½ tsp (2 mL) black pepper

½ tsp (2 mL) paprika

¼ tsp (1 mL) garlic powder

Rimmed baking sheet, lined with parchment paper

1. Preheat the oven to 400°F (200°C).

2. Place the sweet potato, Brussels sprouts, carrots and potato in a large bowl. Drizzle with the oil and sprinkle with salt, pepper, paprika and garlic powder; toss to coat.

3. Spread out the vegetables on the prepared baking sheet in a single layer. Bake in the preheated oven for 20 minutes, until starting to turn golden. Remove from the oven, stir, and bake for another 15 to 20 minutes, until golden brown all over and fork-tender. Remove from the oven; serve.

My Tip

I love using purple carrots to add even more color to this dish. If you can't find purple carrots, regular carrots or parsnips will work.

Cheesy Toasted Garlic Bread

• SERVES 4 • • TIME: 15 MINUTES •

True story: I didn't really appreciate the beauty that is garlic bread until I started making my own. I think a huge draw for me is the way it makes the kitchen smell — the toasty, garlicky, buttery aroma gets me every time. I make it with a sprinkle of vegan cheese and serve it with Untraditional "Chicken" Parmesan (page 156) or Red Pepper Fettuccini (page 170) for an Italian-inspired meal.

¼ cup (60 mL) vegan butter

1 tsp (5 mL) garlic powder

8 slices bread

½ tsp (2 mL) dried parsley

½ cup (125 mL) vegan Cheddar- or mozzarella-style cheese shreds

Rimmed baking sheet, lined with foil

1. Preheat the oven to Broil, with the rack positioned 4 inches (10 cm) from the heat.

2. Combine the vegan butter and garlic powder in a small bowl. Heat in the microwave in 10- to 15-second intervals until the butter is melted.

3. Arrange the bread slices in a single layer on the prepared baking sheet. Drizzle 1½ tsp (7 mL) melted garlic butter over each slice and spread it around with a spoon. Sprinkle equal amounts of parsley and vegan cheese over each piece.

4. Broil for about 5 minutes, until the cheese is melted and the bread is golden brown and crispy. Watch it closely, because it could burn! Remove from the oven and serve.

My Tip

I love using thick slices of crusty bread from a local bakery to make this recipe. I usually make it the same day I buy the bread, so it's super soft, with a nice crisp crust.

Roasted Mini Potatoes with Basil Cream

• SERVES 4 • 🕐 🍴 • TIME: 40 MINUTES (PLUS 1 HOUR FOR SOAKING IF YOU DON'T HAVE A HIGH-POWERED BLENDER) •

If you are a fan of pesto, you will die for these crispy roasted potatoes with their creamy garlic and basil pesto-inspired sauce.

Basil Cream

- ¾ cup (175 mL) raw cashews
- ½ cup (125 mL) water
- ½ cup (125 mL) packed fresh basil leaves
- 1 garlic clove (see My Tip)
- 1½ tbsp (22 mL) freshly squeezed lemon juice

Potatoes

- 1½ lbs (750 g) yellow mini potatoes, halved
- 1 tbsp (15 mL) olive oil

- 1 tsp (5 mL) paprika
- ½ tsp (2 mL) salt
- ¼ tsp (1 mL) freshly ground black pepper
- 2 tbsp (30 mL) chopped fresh basil or flat-leaf (Italian) parsley (optional)

Rimmed baking sheet, lined with parchment paper

High-powered blender or food processor

1. **BASIL CREAM:** If you don't have a high-powered blender, soak the cashews for 1 hour in a small bowl with enough hot water to cover. Drain. (Proceed to Step 2 if you are using a high-powered blender.)

2. **POTATOES:** Preheat the oven to 400°F (200°C).

3. Combine the potatoes, oil, paprika, salt and pepper in a large bowl; toss to coat. Place on the prepared baking sheet in a single layer. Bake in the preheated oven for 30 minutes, stirring halfway through, until golden brown and fork-tender.

4. **BASIL CREAM:** Meanwhile, combine the cashews, water, basil, garlic and lemon juice in the blender or food processor. Blend on high speed for 1 minute or until smooth and creamy.

5. Remove potatoes from oven. Transfer to a bowl and serve with the sauce drizzled overtop or on the side for dipping. Garnish with fresh basil or parsley (if using).

My Tip
You can use ¼ tsp (1 mL) garlic powder instead of the garlic clove, if desired.

Super-Fluffy Mashed Potatoes

• SERVES 4 • • TIME: 20 MINUTES •

It's really easy to make amazing vegan mashed potatoes by simply replacing the butter and milk with vegan versions. I make this fluffy mash for all my holiday meals, and I promise you there will never be any leftovers. I suggest serving them with Veggie Gravy (page 13) for the optimal mashed-potato experience.

5 large russet potatoes (about 2½ lbs), peeled and cut into chunks

3 tbsp (45 mL) vegan butter or vegan margarine

¼ cup (60 mL) unsweetened nondairy milk

¼ tsp (1 mL) salt (approx.)

¼ tsp (1 mL) black pepper (approx.)

1. Place the potatoes in a large pot and cover with about 2 inches (5 cm) of water. Bring to a boil over high heat, then reduce the heat and boil gently for about 15 minutes, until fork-tender. Drain and return to the pot.

2. Add the vegan butter, nondairy milk, salt and pepper. Using a potato masher or fork, mash the potatoes until smooth. Taste and add extra salt or pepper if desired. Transfer to a serving bowl and serve.

Cajun-Spiced Wedges

• SERVES 4 • • TIME: 45 MINUTES •

This recipe is one of my go-tos when I have friends over to watch a movie. It's great for serving with an array of dipping sauces that you can put in cute little dishes. I love to serve ketchup, sweet chili sauce and Vegan "Honey Mustard" Dip (page 17).

2 tsp (10 mL) paprika

1 tsp (5 mL) salt

1 tsp (5 mL) black pepper

½ tsp (2 mL) garlic powder

¼ tsp (1 mL) onion powder

¾ tsp (3 mL) hot pepper flakes

2 lbs (1 kg) white potatoes, cut into wedges

2 tbsp (30 mL) olive oil

Rimmed baking sheet, lined with parchment paper

1. Preheat the oven to 425°F (220°C).

2. Stir together the paprika, salt, pepper, garlic powder, onion powder and hot pepper flakes in a small bowl. Set aside.

3. Place the potatoes in a large bowl. Add the oil and toss to coat. Add the spice mixture and stir to coat the wedges.

4. Spread on the prepared baking sheet in a single layer. Bake in the preheated oven for 15 minutes, then flip and bake for 15 minutes more, until golden brown and crispy.

5. Remove from the oven and transfer to a large bowl or plate. Serve with your favorite dipping sauces, if desired.

My Tip

Sometimes it's fun to change up these potatoes by cutting them like traditional french fries. To do this, slice a potato in half lengthwise. Lay each half cut side down and cut lengthwise into ½-inch (1 cm) thick slices. Cut each slice lengthwise into sticks about ¼ inch (0.5 cm) thick. Reduce the cooking time by 5 minutes and keep an eye on them at the end of the baking time, so they don't burn.

Baked Sweet Potato Fries with Curry Mayo

• SERVES 4 • • TIME: 45 MINUTES •

I frequently have arguments with people about whether sweet potato fries or regular fries are better. The thing is, I still can't decide myself! I think they are both good in their own right and should be treated as equals, but I'm a sucker for sweet potato fries and would be hard-pressed to ever turn them down. I typically have these with the curry mayo, but if you are serving them to friends and family, I suggest also making a batch of Spicy Lime Mayo (page 18) as an optional dipping sauce.

Fries

4 large sweet potatoes, peeled and cut into ½-inch (1 cm) thick sticks

¼ cup (60 mL) olive oil

1 tsp (5 mL) salt

½ tsp (2 mL) freshly ground black pepper

Curry Mayo

⅓ cup (75 mL) vegan mayonnaise

1½ tsp (7 mL) curry powder

½ tsp (2 mL) pure maple syrup (optional)

Rimmed baking sheet, lined with parchment paper

1. **FRIES:** Preheat the oven to 425°F (220°C).

2. Place the sweet potatoes in a large bowl. Drizzle with the oil and sprinkle with salt and pepper; toss to coat.

3. Spread the sweet potatoes on the prepared baking sheet in a single layer. Bake in the preheated oven for 15 minutes, then flip and bake for another 15 minutes, until fork-tender and starting to crisp at the edges.

4. **CURRY MAYO:** Meanwhile, whisk together the vegan mayonnaise, curry powder and maple syrup (if using) until combined.

5. Remove the potatoes from the oven; serve the curry mayo alongside for dipping.

Crispy Baked Onion Rings

• SERVES 4 • 🍽 • TIME: 50 MINUTES (PLUS 30 MINUTES FOR SOAKING) •

Don't get me wrong, I love a basket of crispy fried onion rings from a pub, but I actually prefer this recipe, because they are baked and don't make me feel like falling asleep afterward! If you are looking for a new way to eat onion rings, try putting a few on top of your next burger or salad. I serve these with Spicy Lime Mayo (page 18) and ketchup for dipping.

2 cups (500 mL) unsweetened nondairy milk

6 tbsp (90 mL) white vinegar

2 large onions, sliced into ½-inch (1 cm) rings

⅔ cup (150 mL) cornmeal

⅔ cup (150 mL) all-purpose flour

⅔ cup (150 mL) panko bread crumbs

2 tbsp (30 mL) nutritional yeast

1 tsp (5 mL) paprika

½ tsp (2 mL) salt

½ tsp (2 mL) black pepper

Cooking spray (see My Tip)

Rimmed baking sheet, greased

1. Combine the nondairy milk and vinegar in a large bowl. The nondairy milk will curdle, but don't worry — this is supposed to happen. Add the onion rings and soak for 30 minutes. (You can skip the soaking step if you are in a rush, but it helps soften the onions and makes the rings perfectly tender on the inside.)

2. Preheat the oven to 400°F (200°C).

3. Combine the cornmeal, flour, bread crumbs, nutritional yeast, paprika, salt and pepper in a medium bowl.

4. Remove one onion ring from the soaking bowl and dip it in the dry mixture, ensuring that it is completely coated. Place on the prepared baking sheet. Repeat with the remaining onion rings making a single layer.

5. Spritz the onions with cooking spray and bake in the preheated oven for 15 minutes, until golden brown on one side. Remove from the oven, flip and spritz again. Bake for another 10 minutes, until golden brown.

6. Remove from the oven and serve hot with your favorite dipping sauces.

My Tip
If you do not wish to use cooking spray, you can simply bake the onion rings without it, but they will not turn golden brown. I don't recommend trying to brush them with oil before baking, since that can remove the coating.

Sandwiches,
Wraps & Salads

Buffalo Chickpea Wraps

• SERVES 4 • ⬭ • TIME: 10 MINUTES •

I made a recipe very similar to this one for a video on school lunch ideas two years ago. People still send me photos and messages about how they continue to make it regularly!

1 tsp (5 mL) olive oil

1 can (14 oz/398 mL) chickpeas, drained and rinsed

¼ tsp (1 mL) black pepper

¼ cup (60 mL) vegan Buffalo sauce

¼ cup (60 mL) vegan BBQ sauce

2 tbsp (30 mL) vegan mayonnaise

4 large tortillas

2 cups (500 mL) shredded lettuce

1 medium tomato, sliced

1 red onion, sliced

1. Heat a frying pan over medium heat. Add the oil, chickpeas and black pepper; cook for 3 to 4 minutes, stirring frequently, until heated through.

2. Add the vegan Buffalo sauce and vegan BBQ sauce; stir to combine. Simmer for another 5 minutes, stirring constantly, until the sauce has thickened. Remove from the heat and let cool slightly.

3. Spread 1½ tsp (7 mL) vegan mayonnaise over one tortilla. Place about ½ cup (125 mL) of the chickpea mixture along the center, followed by ½ cup (125 mL) shredded lettuce and a quarter of the sliced tomato and onion. Fold the bottom half of the tortilla over the filling. Fold in the sides, then roll it up to close like a burrito. Repeat with the remaining ingredients. Serve.

My Tip

The chickpea mixture can be stored in an airtight container in the fridge for up to 3 days. Reheat it in the microwave just before assembling the wraps.

Gooey Grilled Cheese Sandwiches

• SERVES 4 ♡ TIME: 15 MINUTES •

Grilled cheese sandwiches are something that people often think are off limits when you go vegan, but there are so many ways to make a really good vegan version. Apart from the many vegan cheese options popping up in stores, you can also use homemade vegan cheese. I love to use my Almond Ricotta (page 20) — it's soft and gooey and doesn't require melting. I mix it with chopped baby spinach because it looks fancier and I like sneaking some greens in. As a bonus, this sandwich contains healthy protein, fats and fiber because the cheese is made with almonds.

¾ cup (175 mL) Almond Ricotta (page 20)

1 cup (250 mL) chopped baby spinach

8 slices whole-grain bread

2 tbsp (30 mL) vegan margarine (approx.)

1 tomato, sliced

1. Combine the almond ricotta and spinach in a medium bowl.

2. Heat a large frying pan over medium heat.

3. Spread about ¾ tsp (3 mL) vegan margarine on one side of each slice of bread. Arrange 4 slices, unbuttered sides up, and spread 3 tbsp (45 mL) of the almond ricotta mixture on each. Evenly divide the tomato slices and place on top. Top with the remaining 4 slices of bread, buttered sides out.

4. Working in batches as necessary, place the sandwiches in the preheated frying pan and cook for 3 to 4 minutes per side or until golden brown. Serve immediately.

My Tip

This recipe is a great way to use up any leftover vegan ricotta you might have on hand.

Sweet Sriracha Cauliflower Wraps

• SERVES 4 • • TIME: 35 MINUTES •

This recipe was totally accidental. I was developing a ranch dip but it turned out more like a sauce. Instead of remaking it, I decided to use it and some of my Sweet Sriracha Roasted Cauliflower in a wrap. I loved it so much I knew I had to put it in this book!

Sweet Sriracha Cauliflower Wraps

1 recipe Sweet Sriracha Roasted Cauliflower (page 109)

4 large flour tortillas

2 cups (500 mL) shredded romaine lettuce

1 tomato, sliced or diced

1 ripe avocado, sliced

Ranch Sauce

3 tbsp (45 mL) vegan mayonnaise

¼ cup (60 mL) unsweetened nondairy milk

½ tsp (2 mL) apple cider vinegar

¼ tsp (1 mL) garlic powder

¼ tsp (1 mL) freshly ground black pepper

1 tbsp (15 mL) chopped fresh flat-leaf parsley (optional)

1. **SWEET SRIRACHA CAULIFLOWER WRAPS:** Make Sweet Sriracha Roasted Cauliflower according to the recipe directions on page 109.

2. **RANCH SAUCE:** Meanwhile, whisk together the vegan mayonnaise, nondairy milk, apple cider vinegar, garlic powder, black pepper and parsley (if using).

3. **ASSEMBLY:** Spread about 2 tbsp (30 mL) ranch sauce in the center of each tortilla. Evenly divide the lettuce, tomato, avocado and Sriracha cauliflower and place along the center of each tortilla. Fold the bottom half of the tortilla over the filling. Fold in the sides, then roll it up to close like a burrito. Serve.

My Tip

You can store the cooked cauliflower in an airtight container in the fridge for up to 3 days. Store the sauce in a separate container in the fridge. Reheat the cauliflower in the microwave and assemble the wraps right before eating.

BBQ Tofu-Stuffed Pita Pockets

• SERVES 4 • ⬤ • TIME: 20 MINUTES •

Not to sound . . . well, basic, but as a vegan I almost always have leftover tofu and a few veggies lingering in my fridge, and it can be a challenge figuring out creative ways to use them up. This recipe came about in a clean-out-the-fridge moment. To say I was pleasantly surprised with the result is an understatement, since it's now in this book!

1 tbsp (15 mL) olive oil

½ cup (125 mL) chopped white onion

12 oz (375 g) firm tofu, pressed and cubed (see page 4)

½ cup (125 mL) vegan BBQ sauce

2 medium pita pockets, halved

¼ cup (60 mL) vegan mayonnaise

2 cups (500 mL) shredded romaine lettuce

1 large carrot, shredded

1 cup (250 mL) alfalfa sprouts or microgreens

1. Heat a large frying pan over medium heat for 30 seconds. Add the oil and onion and cook for about 5 minutes, stirring frequently, until translucent. Add the tofu cubes and cook for 3 minutes, stirring occasionally, until beginning to brown.

2. Reduce the heat to medium-low. Add the vegan BBQ sauce and stir to combine. Cook for 5 minutes, stirring frequently, until the tofu is coated and the sauce has thickened slightly. Remove from the heat.

3. Evenly divide the vegan mayonnaise, lettuce, carrot, sprouts and tofu among the 4 pita halves. Serve immediately.

My Tip

The tofu in its sauce can be stored in an airtight container in the fridge for up to 4 days. Reheat it in the microwave just before serving. Store the other ingredients separately and assemble the pitas just before serving.

Chickpea Tuna Pita Pockets

• SERVES 4 • • TIME: 10 MINUTES •

I was never a fan of tuna salad, but since going vegan and trying this mock version made of chickpeas, I'm hooked! (Pun intended.) Slightly mashed chickpeas replicate the texture of flaked fish, which appeals to vegans and non-vegans alike. When I'm not taking this with me on the go, I like to grill it in a panini press so the cheese melts and it gets a bit crispy on the outside.

1 can (14 oz/398 mL) chickpeas, drained and rinsed

¼ cup (60 mL) vegan mayonnaise

½ cup (125 mL) shredded carrot

3 tbsp (45 mL) chopped green onion

¼ cup (60 mL) raisins (optional)

¼ tsp (1 mL) black pepper

2 medium whole wheat pita pockets, halved

½ cup (125 mL) vegan Cheddar cheese shreds

2 cups (500 mL) shredded lettuce

1. Combine the chickpeas and vegan mayonnaise in a large bowl. Using a potato masher or fork, mash the chickpeas until chunky and only a few whole beans remain. Make sure not to over-mash, or it will become mushy.

2. Add the carrot, green onion, raisins (if using) and black pepper; stir to combine.

3. Stuff each pita half with about 2 tbsp (30 mL) of the vegan cheese, then evenly divide the shredded lettuce and the chickpea mixture among the 4 halves. Serve.

My Tip
The chickpea mixture can be stored in an airtight container in the fridge for up to 4 days. When ready to make the pita pockets, reheat it in the microwave until warmed through.

Strawberry Spinach Salad with Buttermilk-Style Dressing

• SERVES 4 • • TIME: 10 MINUTES •

I used to be someone who believed fruit and vegetable salads should be kept separate, without encroaching on each other's territory. After going vegan and experimenting more in the kitchen, I decided that fruit not only belongs in green salads, it takes them to a whole new level. This strawberry spinach salad is the perfect summer side dish, thanks to fresh, ripe strawberries and a creamy buttermilk-inspired dressing.

Buttermilk-Style Dressing

½ cup (125 mL) vegan mayonnaise

2 tbsp (30 mL) unsweetened nondairy milk

2 tbsp (30 mL) apple cider vinegar

2 tbsp (30 mL) organic cane sugar

Salt and freshly ground black pepper

Strawberry Spinach Salad

5 cups (1.25 L) baby spinach

1½ cups (375 mL) sliced fresh strawberries

¾ cup (175 mL) Maple Cinnamon Pecans (page 77), chopped

1. **BUTTERMILK-STYLE DRESSING:** Whisk together the vegan mayonnaise, nondairy milk, apple cider vinegar, sugar and a sprinkle of salt and pepper. Taste and adjust the salt and pepper as needed.

2. **STRAWBERRY SPINACH SALAD:** Combine the spinach, strawberries and pecans in a large bowl; toss to combine. Drizzle the dressing overtop and toss to coat. Serve.

My Tip
Store the salad and dressing separately in airtight containers in the fridge for up to 3 days. Add the dressing just before serving.

Sweet Potato Salad with Spiced Maple Dressing

• SERVES 4 •   • TIME: 40 MINUTES •

This recipe was inspired by the restaurant La Panthère Verte, which I visit every time I go to Montreal. I always have to get their sweet potato salad, and when I return home and the craving hits, I like to make this version for myself.

Sweet Potato Salad

2 large sweet potatoes, peeled and chopped

3 tbsp (45 mL) olive oil

½ tsp (2 mL) salt

¼ tsp (1 mL) pepper

3 cups (750 mL) baby spinach

½ cup (125 mL) pecan halves

½ cup (125 mL) dried cranberries

3 green onions, thinly sliced

Spiced Maple Dressing

⅓ cup (75 mL) olive oil

¼ cup (60 mL) pure maple syrup or agave nectar

1 tbsp (15 mL) freshly squeezed lemon juice

½ tsp (2 mL) ground ginger

¼ tsp (1 mL) ground cinnamon

Rimmed baking sheet, lined with parchment paper

1. **SWEET POTATO SALAD:** Preheat the oven to 400°F (200°C).

2. Combine the sweet potatoes, oil, salt and pepper in a medium bowl. Spread out the pieces evenly on the prepared baking sheet. Bake in the preheated oven for 30 minutes, flipping halfway through, until tender and golden (keep an eye on them to ensure the edges don't burn). Remove from the oven and set aside.

3. **SPICED MAPLE DRESSING:** Meanwhile, whisk together the oil, maple syrup, lemon juice, ginger and cinnamon, until well combined.

4. **ASSEMBLY:** Place the spinach, pecans, dried cranberries, baked sweet potatoes and green onions in a large salad bowl. Pour the dressing overtop and toss to coat.

Thai Spiral Noodle Salad

I can never say no to noodles — especially fun curly noodles made from vegetables and smothered in a creamy, tangy Thai-inspired sauce. If you don't have a spiralizer, you can make this salad by using a vegetable peeler to slice the carrots and zucchini into long ribbons. I did it that way before I got a spiralizer, and it still works great.

8 oz (250 g) rice noodles

1 recipe Thai Peanut Sauce (page 16)

3 large carrots, spiralized or sliced into ribbons

2 medium zucchini, spiralized or sliced into ribbons

1 cup (250 mL) thinly sliced cabbage

4 green onions, sliced

2 tsp (10 mL) black sesame seeds

Spiralizer (optional)

1. Cook the rice noodles according to the package directions. Drain and set aside.

2. Prepare the Thai Peanut Sauce according to the recipe instructions on page 16.

3. Combine the cooked noodles, carrots, zucchini, cabbage, green onions and sesame seeds in a large bowl. Drizzle the sauce overtop and toss to combine. Serve immediately or store in an airtight container in the fridge for up to 3 days.

Basil, Tomato and Parmesan Pasta Salad

• SERVES 4 • • TIME: 20 MINUTES •

Pasta salad is one of those perfect recipes — it travels well and also impresses at a barbecue or potluck. This version is bursting with flavor from the basil, fresh tomatoes and almond Parmesan cheese. Short pasta shapes work best for pasta salad, and bowties are always my first choice.

Pasta Salad

10 oz (300 g) bowtie pasta

1 cucumber, diced

2 cups (500 mL) baby spinach, chopped

2 cups (500 mL) diced fresh Roma (plum) or halved cherry tomatoes

⅓ cup (75 mL) finely chopped fresh basil

Lemon Vinaigrette

⅓ cup (75 mL) olive oil

2 tbsp (30 mL) freshly squeezed lemon juice

1 tsp (5 mL) white vinegar

2 tsp (10 mL) organic cane sugar

½ tsp (2 mL) salt

½ tsp (2 mL) freshly ground black pepper

Almond Parmesan

½ cup (125 mL) slivered almonds

2 tbsp (30 mL) nutritional yeast

⅛ tsp (0.5 mL) salt

⅛ tsp (0.5 mL) garlic powder

Blender or food processor

1. **PASTA SALAD:** Cook the pasta according to the package directions. Drain and set aside.

2. **LEMON VINAIGRETTE:** Meanwhile, whisk together the oil, lemon juice, vinegar, sugar, salt and black pepper in a small bowl. Set aside.

3. **ALMOND PARMESAN:** Combine the almonds, nutritional yeast, salt and garlic powder in a blender or food processor; pulse until the mixture resembles powdered Parmesan cheese.

4. Combine the cooked pasta, cucumber, spinach, tomatoes and basil in a large bowl. Pour the dressing overtop and stir to combine. Sprinkle the almond Parmesan overtop and stir to combine. Serve immediately or store in an airtight container in the fridge for up to 3 days.

Broccoli Quinoa Salad with Creamy Cashew Dressing

· SERVES 4 · · TIME: 25 MINUTES ·

Quinoa is gluten-free and high in protein, and it contains all nine essential amino acids. I use it as a substitute for rice when serving stir-fries and curries, but it also works really well in salads. This recipe is one of my favorites, and it tastes great warm or cold. I usually serve it warm for dinner and then eat the leftovers as a chilled salad the next day. I also like to switch up the dressing: sometimes I use cashew butter for a creamy but milder flavor, and other times I use tahini for a slightly more bitter taste. It's a very adaptable recipe all round.

Broccoli Quinoa Salad

1¼ cups (300 mL) quinoa, rinsed

4 cups (1 L) broccoli florets

2 medium carrots, shredded

½ cup (125 mL) sliced almonds

Creamy Cashew Dressing

¼ cup (60 mL) cashew butter
or tahini

2 tbsp (30 mL) freshly squeezed
lemon juice

1 tsp (5 mL) Dijon mustard

1 garlic clove, minced

1 tsp (5 mL) pure maple syrup
or agave nectar

2 tbsp (30 mL) olive oil

Steamer basket

1. **BROCCOLI QUINOA SALAD:** Cook the quinoa according to the package directions. Fluff and transfer to a large salad bowl.

2. Meanwhile, fill a large pot with 2 inches (5 cm) of water and bring it to a boil over high heat. Fit a steamer basket over the top and place the broccoli inside. Cover and steam for about 5 minutes, until fork-tender. Set aside to cool.

3. **CREAMY CASHEW DRESSING:** Whisk together the cashew butter, lemon juice, Dijon mustard, garlic, maple syrup and oil.

4. Add the cooked broccoli florets, carrots and sliced almonds to the quinoa. Pour the dressing over the salad and toss to combine. Serve immediately or store in an airtight container in the fridge for up to 3 days.

Simple Apple and Kale Salad

· SERVES 4 · · TIME: 10 MINUTES ·

A lot of people don't eat kale because it can be bitter and tough to chew. The key is to massage it with something acidic like lemon juice so it becomes softer and more palatable — which I do in this recipe. This salad is super easy and has pops of sweetness from the fruit. It can be made up to a day in advance, which gives the kale more time to soften and become more flavorful.

3 tbsp (45 mL) freshly squeezed lemon juice

3 tbsp (45 mL) olive oil

6 cups (1.5 L) chopped kale, ribs removed

⅓ cup (75 mL) dried cranberries

1 Granny Smith or Honeycrisp apple, thinly sliced

⅓ cup (75 mL) chopped walnuts

1 recipe Almond Parmesan (page 140)

1. Whisk together the lemon juice and oil in a small bowl.

2. Put the kale in a large bowl. Drizzle the lemon juice mixture overtop. Using your hands, squeeze and massage the kale until it's coated in the dressing and starts to soften slightly, about 2 minutes.

3. Add the cranberries, apple, walnuts and almond Parmesan to the salad; toss to combine. Serve immediately or store in an airtight container in the fridge for up to 2 days.

Summery Quinoa Salad

• SERVES 4 • • TIME: 20 MINUTES (PLUS 1 HOUR FOR CHILLING) •

A fresh chilled quinoa salad reminds me of picnics in Halifax's Point Pleasant Park. You'll often find me there on a summer afternoon with a jar of lemonade, this cucumber quinoa salad, and a bunch of Chewy Chocolate Chip Cookies (page 193). I took my inspiration from a store-bought quinoa salad that I used to buy regularly. I loved the combination of simple flavors and started recreating it at home — and this version is much cheaper than buying it from a store!

1¼ cups (300 mL) quinoa, rinsed

1 can (14 oz/398 mL) brown lentils, drained and rinsed

1 large cucumber, chopped

1 red bell pepper, finely chopped

½ cup (125 mL) finely chopped fresh flat-leaf (Italian) parsley

¼ cup (60 mL) olive oil

¼ cup (60 mL) freshly squeezed lemon juice

1 garlic clove, minced

¼ tsp (1 mL) salt

1. Cook the quinoa according to the package directions. Fluff and transfer to a large bowl. Add the lentils, cucumber, bell pepper and parsley.

2. Whisk together the oil, lemon juice, garlic and salt in a small bowl. Drizzle over the salad and toss to combine. Cover and transfer to the fridge to chill for at least 1 hour before serving.

My Tip

Store the salad in an airtight container in the fridge for up to 3 days.

Caesar Salad with Garlicky Croutons

• SERVES 4 • • TIME: 20 MINUTES •

Croutons are the key ingredient in this salad, and I was late learning how fast and easy it is to make your own. They definitely taste better than the ones I used to buy in a package! It's a great way to use up bread that's a few days old, so I like to make this salad near the end of the week.

Croutons

2 cups (500 mL) cubed bread or baguette

¼ cup (60 mL) vegan butter, melted

¼ tsp (1 mL) garlic powder

Dressing

3 garlic cloves

¼ cup (60 mL) vegan mayonnaise

2 tsp (10 mL) white vinegar

2 tsp (10 mL) Dijon mustard

2 tbsp (30 mL) freshly squeezed lemon juice

¼ tsp (1 mL) freshly ground black pepper

⅓ cup (75 mL) olive oil

Salad

1 large romaine lettuce head, chopped

¼ cup (60 mL) soy bacon bits (optional)

Blender

Rimmed baking sheet

1. Preheat the oven to 350°F (180°C).

2. **CROUTONS:** Place the cubed bread in a large bowl; add the melted vegan butter and garlic powder and toss to coat. Spread in an even layer on the baking sheet. Bake in the preheated oven for 15 minutes, flipping halfway through, until golden brown. Remove from the oven and set aside to cool slightly.

3. **DRESSING:** Meanwhile, combine the garlic, vegan mayonnaise, vinegar, Dijon mustard, lemon juice, pepper and oil in a blender. Blend on high speed for about 1 minute, until smooth.

4. **SALAD:** In a large salad bowl, combine the lettuce, soy bacon bits (if using) and croutons. Add the dressing and gently toss to combine, using two forks or salad tongs. Serve immediately.

Mains

Saucy Seitan Sandwiches

• SERVES 4 ♡ TIME: 10 MINUTES •

I have always loved messy sandwiches overflowing with sauce. Despite the fact that I inevitably stain at least one piece of clothing with barbecue sauce, my love for these sandwiches persists. I often make a batch of Sliceable Seitan (page 25) with the intention of making something new, but time and time again I come back to this recipe because of its simplicity and awesome flavor. I recommend eating this with a side of Cajun-Spiced Wedges (page 121) or Caesar Salad with Garlicky Croutons (page 148).

2 tbsp (30 mL) vegetable oil, divided

½ medium onion, thinly sliced

1 recipe Sliceable Seitan (page 25) or 1½ cups (375 mL) store-bought seitan

¾ cup (175 mL) vegan BBQ sauce

4 burger buns

2 tbsp (30 mL) vegan mayonnaise

Optional Toppings

Sliced vegan cheese

Store-bought vegan coleslaw or sauerkraut

Sliced red onion

Lettuce

1. Heat a medium frying pan over medium heat. Add 1 tbsp (15 mL) oil and the onion and cook for 5 minutes, stirring frequently, until the onion is translucent.

2. Meanwhile, use a knife to chop the seitan into small chunks. Add the remaining 1 tbsp (15 mL) oil and the seitan chunks to the frying pan; cook for 3 minutes, stirring frequently, until the seitan starts to brown. Reduce the heat to low, add the vegan BBQ sauce and stir to coat.

3. Spread 1½ tsp (7 mL) vegan mayo on the top half of each burger bun. Evenly divide the seitan mixture and pile on the bottom half of each bun. Add sliced vegan cheese, coleslaw, red onion and lettuce (if using). Serve immediately.

Spicy "Sausage" Tacos

• SERVES 4 • • TIME: 30 MINUTES •

What vegan cookbook would be complete without a recipe for tacos? This was the first recipe I created using my seitan crumbles, and I love how their savory flavor goes so well with spicy jalapeño pepper in these tacos. I like to combine spicy flavors with something creamy, which is why I recommend using ripe avocado chunks and vegan sour cream. If you'll be hosting a Cinco de Mayo party, you will definitely want to make these, as well as a batch of Cheesy Warm Nachos (page 74)!

1 recipe Seitan "Sausage" Crumbles (page 24) or 11 oz (340 g) store-bought vegan ground beef

½ small head romaine lettuce, shredded

1 jalapeño pepper, seeded and minced

½ cup (125 mL) chopped red onion

1 cup (250 mL) vegan Cheddar cheese shreds

1 ripe avocado, cut into chunks

1 cup (250 mL) store-bought tomato salsa

8 medium corn or flour tortillas

1 cup (250 mL) vegan sour cream (optional)

¼ cup (60 mL) chopped fresh cilantro leaves (optional)

1. Prepare the seitan crumbles according to the recipe on page 24. (If using vegan ground beef, heat it in a frying pan over medium heat for about 5 minutes, stirring frequently, until browned.)

2. Evenly divide the seitan crumbles, lettuce, jalapeño pepper, red onion, vegan Cheddar cheese, avocado and salsa among the tortillas. Spoon the vegan sour cream overtop and sprinkle with cilantro (if using). Serve immediately.

Untraditional "Chicken" Parmesan

• SERVES 4 ⑂ TIME: 30 MINUTES •

Chicken Parmesan is classic comfort food that, thankfully, can be made vegan with a couple of simple substitutions. I use my homemade marinara sauce because I love its chunky texture and fresh flavor, but if you are short on time you can use your favorite store-bought sauce instead. If you are craving chicken Parmesan flavors but don't feel like pasta, you can omit the spaghetti and use the cheesy baked "chicken" cutlets in a sandwich.

3 cups (750 mL) Marinara Sauce (page 12) or store-bought

4 vegan breaded "chicken" cutlets (see My Tip)

1 cup (250 mL) vegan mozzarella shreds

14 oz (400 g) spaghetti

¼ cup (60 mL) Almond Parmesan (page 140) or store-bought vegan Parmesan cheese

2 tbsp (30 mL) chopped fresh flat-leaf (Italian) parsley (optional)

8-inch (20 cm) square baking dish

1. Preheat the oven to 350°F (180°C).

2. Spread about half of the marinara sauce about 1 inch (2.5 cm) thick over bottom of the baking dish. Place the 4 "chicken" cutlets in a single layer on top and cover with the remaining marinara sauce. Bake in the preheated oven for 10 minutes. Sprinkle the vegan mozzarella cheese overtop and bake for another 15 minutes, until the cheese is melted.

3. Meanwhile, cook the spaghetti according to the package directions. Drain and set aside.

4. Remove the baking dish from the oven. Evenly divide the pasta among 4 bowls. Top with marinara sauce from the dish, then add a "chicken" cutlet to each. Evenly sprinkle the vegan Parmesan cheese and fresh parsley (if using) over the top.

My Tip
If you can't find vegan "chicken" cutlets, my Crispy Tofu Dippers (page 69) make a great substitute.

Black Bean and Corn Tacos

• SERVES 4 • • TIME: 15 MINUTES •

This is a great recipe for parties because everyone can customize their own tacos. I like to create a big spread of toppings with lettuce, guacamole, salsa, vegan cheeses, fresh herbs and hot sauce, which is fun for guests and looks impressive.

Black Bean and Corn Filling

1 tsp (5 mL) olive oil

½ onion, chopped

1 bell pepper, chopped

½ cup (125 mL) vegan ground beef (optional)

¾ cup (175 mL) drained and rinsed black beans

½ cup (125 mL) frozen corn kernels

¾ cup (175 mL) store-bought tomato salsa

2 tsp (10 mL) taco seasoning

8 medium corn or flour tortillas

Optional Toppings

3 cups (750 mL) shredded lettuce

1½ cups (375 mL) vegan Cheddar cheese shreds

1 recipe Five-Minute Guacamole (page 78) or 1½ cups (375 mL) store-bought

1 cup (250 mL) vegan sour cream or Spicy Lime Mayo (page 18)

Hot sauce

Chopped fresh cilantro

1. Heat a large frying pan over medium heat. Add the oil, onion and bell pepper; cook for 5 minutes, stirring frequently, until the onion becomes translucent. Add the vegan ground beef (if using), black beans, corn, salsa and taco seasoning; cook for 5 minutes, stirring frequently, until thickened slightly.

2. Evenly divide the filling among the tortillas. Top with lettuce, vegan Cheddar cheese, guacamole, vegan sour cream or Spicy Lime Mayo, hot sauce and fresh cilantro (if using). Serve immediately.

My Tip
For even more budget-friendly tacos, skip the vegan ground beef and vegan cheese and use my homemade guacamole (page 78) instead.

Lentil Chili

• SERVES 4 • • TIME: 1 HOUR 15 MINUTES •

This chili is packed with veggies and lentils, which give you a good dose of fiber and protein, making it both healthy and filling. I use no-salt-added broth and tomatoes so that I can add my own salt and control the amount of sodium in my chili. Serve this with a salad like my Caesar (page 148) and some fresh bread on the side for dipping.

2 tbsp (30 mL) olive oil

1 medium white onion, diced

1 medium zucchini, chopped

1 large red bell pepper, chopped

1 carrot, chopped

2 cups (500 mL) no-salt-added vegetable broth

2 cans (each 28 oz/796 mL) no-salt-added diced tomatoes (with juice)

¾ cup (175 mL) dried brown lentils, rinsed

3 tbsp (45 mL) chili powder (approx.)

2 tsp (10 mL) ground coriander

1 tsp (5 mL) salt (approx.)

½ tsp (2 mL) black pepper (approx.)

1 ripe avocado, cut into chunks (optional)

1. Heat a large pot over medium heat. Add the oil and onion and cook for 5 minutes, stirring frequently, until translucent. Add the zucchini, bell pepper and carrot; cook for 5 minutes, stirring frequently, until softened.

2. Add the vegetable broth, tomatoes (with juice), lentils, chili powder, coriander, salt and pepper; stir to combine. Increase the heat to medium-high and bring to a light boil, then immediately reduce the heat to medium-low. Simmer for 1 hour, stirring occasionally, until the lentils are tender and the chili has thickened. Add more chili powder, salt and pepper if desired.

3. Divide among 4 bowls and top with avocado chunks (if using); serve.

My Tip

If you have leftovers, they can be stored in an airtight container in the fridge for up to 4 days or in the freezer for up to 2 months.

Hawaiian-ish Pizza

• SERVES 4 • • TIME: 25 MINUTES •

I started out my pizza-eating days firmly believing that pineapple had no place on a pizza. But after going vegan I started to love a little bit of sweetness on my pizza, and now it is a full-blown obsession. I understand that the world is pretty divided on this topic, so forgive me if this recipe offends you. But I still think you should give it a chance, because it's really tasty!

2 12-inch (30 cm) pizza crusts

2 cups (500 mL) store-bought pizza sauce (see My Tip)

3 cups (750 mL) vegan mozzarella cheese shreds

1 red bell pepper, thinly sliced

½ red onion, thinly sliced

1 recipe Seitan "Sausage" Crumbles (page 24) or 11 oz (340 g) store-bought vegan ground beef

1 cup (250 mL) chopped or sliced pineapple

⅔ cup (150 mL) vegan BBQ sauce (approx.)

Round baking sheet or pizza stone

1. Working with one pizza crust at a time, place a crust on the baking sheet or pizza stone. Spread 1 cup (250 mL) pizza sauce over the crust, smoothing it into an even layer with the back of a spoon. Sprinkle 1½ cups (375 mL) vegan mozzarella shreds evenly overtop. Add half the bell pepper, onion, seitan crumbles and pineapple. Drizzle ⅓ cup (75 mL) vegan BBQ sauce overtop.

2. Bake according to the pizza crust instructions. Repeat with the second pizza crust. Slice and serve.

My Tip

Most store-bought pizza sauces are vegan, but if you have any doubts about a certain brand, check the ingredients to be sure.

Caprese Pizza

Pizza is a classic food that people often miss when they go vegan. This one reminds me of a caprese salad, thanks to the fresh basil, tomato and little pockets of creamy, tangy ricotta. I always add spinach and fresh basil because they are super good for you and add a beautiful pop of vibrant green.

2 12-inch (30 cm) pizza crusts

2 cups (500 mL) store-bought vegan pizza sauce

1½ cups (375 mL) chopped baby spinach

1 large ripe tomato, sliced

1 recipe Almond Ricotta (page 20) or Tofu Ricotta (page 21) or 3 cups (750 mL) vegan mozzarella shreds

½ cup (125 mL) chopped fresh basil

Round baking sheet or pizza stone

1. Working with one pizza crust at a time, place a crust on the baking sheet or pizza stone. Pour 1 cup (250 mL) pizza sauce over the crust and smooth it into an even layer with the back of a spoon. Add ¾ cup (175 mL) spinach, followed by half the tomato slices. Drop half of the ricotta in small spoonfuls, each ½ to 1 tsp (2 to 5 mL), evenly over the pizza, or sprinkle 1½ cups (375 mL) vegan mozzarella shreds in an even layer. Sprinkle fresh basil overtop.

2. Bake according to the pizza crust instructions. Repeat with the remaining crust. Remove from the oven, slice and serve.

Chickpea, Lentil and Sweet Potato Curry

• SERVES 4 • • TIME: 35 MINUTES •

It's good to have a hearty curry recipe in your back pocket when fall and winter roll around, although I actually enjoy eating this recipe any time of the year. For a balanced and filling meal, I love to eat this curry with a grain such as rice or quinoa.

2 tbsp (30 mL) vegetable oil

1 cup (250 mL) chopped onion

2 garlic cloves, minced

1½ tbsp (22 mL) mild curry powder

1 medium sweet potato, peeled and diced

1 can (14 oz/398 mL) brown lentils, drained and rinsed

1 can (14 oz/398 mL) cooked chickpeas, drained and rinsed

1 can (28 oz/796 mL) diced tomatoes (with juice)

1 can (14 oz/398 mL) full-fat coconut milk

Salt

Pepper

Optional for Serving

Hot cooked basmati rice, brown rice or quinoa

Lime wedges

1. Heat a large pot over medium heat. Add the oil, onion and garlic; cook for 5 minutes, stirring frequently, until the onion is translucent. Reduce the heat to medium-low and add the curry powder, sweet potato, lentils, chickpeas, tomatoes (with juice), coconut milk and salt and pepper to taste. Simmer for 20 to 25 minutes, stirring occasionally, until the sweet potato is fork-tender. Add salt and pepper, if desired; stir to combine.

2. Serve hot over your choice of grains (if using) or enjoy the curry on its own with lime wedges to squeeze overtop, if desired.

Mac and Cheese Bake

• SERVES 4 • • TIME: 40 MINUTES •

I have never met anyone who doesn't like mac and cheese. However, I have met people who claim they don't like *vegan* mac and cheese. While I understand that there are some questionable vegan cheese substitutes out there, I encourage you to try my homemade version. I spread my gooey, cheesy sauce all over the macaroni and bake it with some bread crumbs on top to get a nice crispy crust. I promise it will surprise even the biggest cheese-lovers!

14 oz (400 g) macaroni

1 recipe Cheese Sauce (page 19) or 2 cups (500 mL) store-bought vegan cheese sauce

1 cup (250 mL) vegan Cheddar cheese shreds

½ cup (125 mL) panko bread crumbs

1 tsp (5 mL) hot pepper flakes

½ tsp (2 mL) freshly ground black pepper

10-cup (2.5 L) casserole dish

1. Preheat the oven to 350°F (180°C).

2. Meanwhile, cook the macaroni according to the package directions. Drain.

3. Add the cooked macaroni to the casserole dish. Pour the cheese sauce overtop and stir to combine. Sprinkle the vegan Cheddar shreds, bread crumbs, hot pepper flakes and pepper evenly overtop. Bake in the preheated oven for 15 minutes or until the cheese is melted and the bread crumbs are golden. Let cool for 5 minutes before serving.

My Tip
You can make this recipe gluten-free by using gluten-free pasta (such as brown rice macaroni) instead of wheat pasta and omitting the bread crumbs or using gluten-free bread crumbs.

Maple Curry Penne

• SERVES 4 ⩔ TIME: 30 MINUTES •

This recipe was inspired by a dish I had at a cute restaurant in New Brunswick called Lily's Café, years ago, before I went vegan. It was quite an easy dish to make plant-based: I only needed to use coconut milk instead of heavy cream and omit the meat. It is a super-popular recipe on my YouTube channel; everyone who tries it adores it as much as I do.

14 oz (400 g) penne pasta

6 tbsp (90 mL) almond butter

2 tbsp (30 mL) tomato paste

¼ cup (60 mL) pure maple syrup

3 tbsp (45 mL) soy sauce

2 tbsp (30 mL) curry powder

2 tbsp (30 mL) freshly squeezed lemon juice

1 cup (250 mL) full-fat coconut milk

1 tbsp (15 mL) olive oil

1 large red bell pepper, thinly sliced

½ medium onion, chopped

1 cup (250 mL) baby spinach

Chopped curly-leaf parsley (optional)

1. Cook the pasta in a large pot according to the package directions. Drain and then put it back in the pot. Set aside.

2. Meanwhile, whisk together the almond butter, tomato paste, maple syrup, soy sauce, curry powder and lemon juice in a medium bowl. Slowly add the coconut milk, whisking constantly until smooth. Set aside.

3. Heat a large frying pan over medium heat. Add the oil, bell pepper and onion. Cook for 5 minutes, stirring frequently, until the onion is translucent and the pepper has softened.

4. Pour the maple curry sauce into the pan, then add the spinach; simmer over low heat for 3 minutes, stirring frequently, until the sauce has thickened. Add to the pasta and stir to coat.

5. Place the pasta pot back on low heat and heat for 2 minutes, constantly stirring gently, until the pasta is warmed through. Serve.

Red Pepper Fettuccini

• SERVES 4 • • TIME: 30 MINUTES •

This is a great weeknight Italian dinner recipe that makes even better leftovers. The peppers add sweetness while the cashews create the most luxurious, creamy sauce. I love serving this fettuccini with a side of Cheesy Toasted Garlic Bread (page 117) and a light salad, like my Strawberry Spinach Salad with Buttermilk-Style Dressing (page 135).

1 tbsp (15 mL) olive oil

½ cup (125 mL) chopped Spanish onion

2 garlic cloves, chopped

3 cups (750 mL) chopped red bell pepper (about 2 large)

10 oz (300 g) fettuccini pasta

¾ cup (175 mL) unsweetened nondairy milk

½ cup (125 mL) raw cashews (see page 4)

½ tsp (2 mL) salt (approx.)

¼ tsp (1 mL) freshly ground black pepper (approx.)

High-powered blender

1. Heat a large frying pan over medium heat. Add the oil, onion and garlic; cook for 3 minutes, stirring frequently. Add the bell peppers; cook for 5 minutes, stirring frequently, until softened. Remove from the heat.

2. Cook the pasta according to the package directions. Drain and set aside.

3. Add the vegetable mixture, nondairy milk and cashews to the blender, setting the frying pan aside. Blend on high speed for about 2 minutes, until smooth and creamy.

4. Pour the sauce back into the frying pan and heat over low heat. Add the salt and pepper; stir to combine. Simmer for 5 to 10 minutes, stirring constantly so the sauce doesn't stick to the bottom, until slightly thickened. Taste and adjust the salt and pepper to your liking.

5. Divide the pasta among 4 bowls and pour equal amounts of the sauce over each.

My Tip

Arborio rice is a short-grain rice that is necessary for making risotto. Unfortunately there are no substitutes.

Lemon Asparagus Risotto

• SERVES 4 • • TIME: 45 MINUTES •

For many people, risotto reminds them of fancy restaurants. The truth is, it isn't difficult or hard to make; it just takes a bit of time. The key to getting risotto super creamy is to add warm broth slowly while the rice is cooking. This gives the rice time to release its starch and create a thick sauce. I like to make risotto when I'm not in a rush and can pour myself a glass of wine and enjoy the process.

4 cups (1 L) low-sodium vegetable broth

2 tbsp (30 mL) olive oil, divided

¼ cup (60 mL) finely chopped onion

10 asparagus spears, trimmed and chopped into 1-inch (2.5 cm) pieces

1¼ cups (300 mL) Arborio rice (see My Tip)

¼ tsp (1 mL) salt (approx.)

¼ tsp (1 mL) pepper

1½ tbsp (22 mL) freshly squeezed lemon juice

Almond Parmesan (page 140) or vegan Parmesan cheese (optional)

Freshly ground black pepper (optional)

1. Heat the vegetable broth in a medium pot over medium heat. Bring to a light simmer for 2 minutes, then reduce the heat to low and keep hot.

2. Heat a large pot over medium heat. Add 1 tbsp (15 mL) oil and the onion and cook for about 5 minutes, stirring frequently, until translucent. Add the asparagus and cook for 3 to 4 minutes, stirring frequently, until softened. Pour the asparagus mixture into a large bowl. Set the bowl aside and return the pot to the stovetop over medium heat.

3. Add the remaining 1 tbsp (15 mL) oil and the rice and cook for 3 minutes, stirring constantly, until golden. Add ½ cup (125 mL) hot broth; stir constantly for about 3 to 4 minutes, until the broth is fully absorbed. Continue adding broth ½ cup (125 mL) at a time, stirring continuously and adjusting the heat as necessary to keep the rice at a gentle simmer, until the rice is al dente, about 30 minutes.

4. Add the salt, pepper and lemon juice; stir to combine. Add the asparagus mixture; stir to combine.

5. Serve hot with a sprinkle of vegan Parmesan cheese and some freshly ground black pepper (if using).

Sweet Chili Tofu and Rice Bowls

• SERVES 4 • • TIME: 35 MINUTES •

I would be rich if I earned a dollar every time I made a tofu and rice bowl. I honestly could eat one every night of the week and never get sick of them! I like to keep my bowls tasting fresh by using cucumber and avocado, but feel free to use carrots, cabbage or other veggies of your choice. This recipe is best eaten right away after making, since the tofu will get less crispy the longer it sits with sauce on it.

1¼ cups (300 mL) white or brown rice

1 recipe Best-Ever Tofu Cubes (page 22)

½ cup (125 mL) sweet chili sauce (see My Tip)

½ large cucumber, sliced into strips

1 ripe avocado, sliced

Sesame seeds (optional)

1 lime, cut into wedges

1. Cook the rice according to the package directions. Set aside.

2. Meanwhile, cook the tofu according to the recipe instructions (page 22).

3. Add the tofu to a large bowl and drizzle with the chili sauce; toss to coat.

4. Divide the rice among 4 bowls. Top with the tofu and sauce, cucumber strips and avocado slices. Garnish with sesame seeds (if using) and lime wedges; serve.

My Tip

Sweet chili sauce is a thick, sweet pourable sauce made with garlic and chili flakes. This popular Thai condiment is, thankfully, easy to find at most grocery stores. It makes an excellent sauce for my crispy tofu cubes and a great dip for spring rolls and potato wedges.

My Tip
For a fun presentation, spoon a quarter of the pad thai mixture into each hollowed-out squash half.

Spaghetti Squash Pad Thai

• SERVES 4 ▽ TIME: 45 MINUTES •

Pad thai is my go-to takeout meal. I make this recipe on days when I'm feeling that I need to get in an extra serving of veggies. The texture of the squash is a nice change from typical rice noodles, and it's packed with beneficial nutrients such as potassium and vitamin A, as well as fiber.

Spaghetti Squash

2 spaghetti squash (each 2½ lbs/ 1.25 kg), halved lengthwise and seeded

2 tbsp (30 mL) vegetable oil, divided

1 recipe Thai Peanut Sauce (page 16)

12 oz (375 g) block firm tofu, cubed

1 red bell pepper, thinly sliced

1 medium carrot, chopped

3 green onions, finely chopped

Optional Toppings

Bean sprouts

Chopped fresh cilantro leaves

Chopped peanuts

Rimmed baking sheet, lined with parchment paper

1. **SPAGHETTI SQUASH:** Preheat the oven to 425°F (220°C).

2. Brush the cut sides of each squash half with 1 tsp (5 mL) oil and place cut side down on the prepared baking sheet. Bake in the preheated oven for 35 minutes, until fork-tender.

3. Meanwhile, make the Thai Peanut Sauce according to the recipe instructions (page 16). Set aside.

4. When the squash has 10 minutes of cooking time remaining, prepare the vegetables and tofu: Heat a large frying over medium heat. Add the remaining 2 tsp (10 mL) oil, tofu, bell pepper and carrot; cook for 5 minutes, stirring frequently, until the vegetables are tender. Add the green onions and cook for 1 minute, until softened. Set aside.

5. Remove the squash from the oven and flip over each half. Using a fork, scrape the inside to loosen the "spaghetti" strands. Scrape the strands into a large serving bowl. Drizzle the peanut sauce overtop and toss to coat. Add the cooked vegetables and tofu and toss until combined. Garnish with bean sprouts, cilantro and peanuts (if using). Serve immediately.

Vegetable Fried Rice

· SERVES 4 ♥ TIME: 30 MINUTES ·

This fried rice is a great meal on its own, thanks to the tofu, but it also makes a satisfying side dish. When I want a full Chinese-inspired meal, I'll serve it with Sweet Chili Tofu (page 174) and Sesame Mixed Vegetables (page 106). This fried rice reheats well, so it makes great leftovers for lunch the next day (see My Tip).

1¼ cups (300 mL) white or brown rice

1 tbsp (15 mL) vegetable oil

8 oz (250 g) firm tofu, crumbled

½ tsp (2 mL) ground turmeric

¼ tsp (1 mL) salt

2 medium carrots, chopped

½ cup (125 mL) frozen green peas

½ cup (125 mL) frozen corn kernels

1 tbsp (15 mL) water

⅓ cup (75 mL) chopped green onions

3 tbsp (45 mL) reduced-sodium soy sauce

1 tsp (5 mL) sesame oil

¼ tsp (1 mL) black pepper

1. Cook the rice according to the package directions. Set aside.

2. Meanwhile, heat a large frying pan or wok over medium heat. Add the vegetable oil, tofu, turmeric and salt. Cook for about 5 minutes, stirring frequently, until the tofu is bright yellow and starting to brown.

3. Add the carrots, peas, corn and water; cover with a lid or baking sheet. Cook for about 8 minutes, lifting the lid to stir frequently, until the carrots are tender. Add the cooked rice, green onions, soy sauce and sesame oil; stir to combine. Cook for another 5 minutes, stirring frequently, until the rice is coated in soy sauce and the flavors have melded.

4. Remove from the heat and add pepper; stir to combine. Transfer to a serving bowl; serve.

My Tip
Store the fried rice in an airtight container in the fridge for up to 3 days. Reheat in the microwave until heated through.

My Tip
This dish is best eaten right away. The noodles will absorb the sauce pretty quickly if left in the fridge overnight, so I don't recommend keeping this for leftovers.

Dragon Noodles

I made this recipe on my YouTube channel a few years ago but it has remained a staple in my kitchen ever since. The key to these noodles is to offset the spiciness of the Sriracha sauce with the richness of vegan butter. I know everyone has a different tolerance when it comes to spiciness, so if you are worried about the amount of heat in this dish, start with half the amounts of Sriracha sauce and hot pepper flakes and add more as you go. And for all you brave souls out there, you may want to add even more spice than I have here!

14 oz (400 g) rice-stick noodles (also sometimes called pad thai noodles)

3 tbsp (45 mL) vegan butter, divided

8 oz (175 g) firm tofu, crumbled

¾ cup (175 mL) sliced green onions, divided

1 red bell pepper, thinly sliced

1 cup (250 mL) thinly sliced cabbage

½ cup (125 mL) reduced-sodium soy sauce

⅓ cup (75 mL) pure maple syrup or brown sugar

2 tbsp (30 mL) Sriracha sauce

1½ tsp (7 mL) hot pepper flakes

Sesame seeds (optional)

1. Cook the rice noodles according to the package directions. Drain and set aside.

2. Heat a large frying pan over medium heat. Add 2 tbsp (30 mL) vegan butter and heat for about 1 minute, until melted. Add the tofu, ½ cup (125 mL) green onions, bell pepper and cabbage; cook for 8 minutes, stirring frequently, until the tofu starts to brown.

3. Combine the soy sauce, maple syrup, Sriracha and hot pepper flakes in a small bowl. Set aside.

4. Add the remaining 1 tbsp (15 mL) vegan butter to the tofu mixture and let it melt. Add the cooked noodles and the soy sauce mixture and stir to coat. Cook for another 1 to 2 minutes, stirring gently, until the sauce thickens.

5. Serve immediately in 4 bowls with a sprinkle of sesame seeds (if using) and the remaining green onions.

Sweets

My Favorite Banana Bread

• MAKES 1 LOAF • ⬭ • TIME: 1 HOUR 15 MINUTES •

Banana bread is a staple that I want everyone to know how to make. You can eat it for breakfast, with some nut butter, or for dessert, with a sprinkle of chocolate chips added to the batter before baking (see My Tip). It tastes best when you use super-ripe, very spotty bananas. Whenever I have some lying around, I know there will be banana bread in my near future.

1¾ cups (425 mL) unbleached all-purpose flour

⅓ cup (75 mL) organic cane sugar

2 tsp (10 mL) baking powder

½ tsp (2 mL) baking soda

4 overripe medium bananas, mashed (about 1¼ cups/300 mL)

¼ cup (60 mL) melted coconut oil

1 tsp (5 mL) vanilla extract

8- by 4-inch (20 by 10 cm) metal loaf pan, lined with parchment paper

1. Preheat the oven to 350°F (180°C).

2. Whisk together the flour, sugar, baking powder and baking soda in a medium bowl, until combined.

3. Place the mashed bananas, coconut oil and vanilla in a large bowl; whisk until combined. Add the flour mixture and stir until just combined.

4. Pour into the prepared pan and bake in the preheated oven for 55 to 60 minutes, until brown and cracked on top and a tester inserted in the center comes out with a few crumbs attached. Let cool completely on a wire rack before removing from the pan. Slice and serve immediately or store in an airtight container in the fridge for up to 5 days.

My Tip

To make chocolate chip banana bread, stir ½ cup (125 mL) vegan chocolate chips into the batter before pouring it into the pan.

Carrot Cake with Cream Cheese Frosting

· SERVES 12 · · TIME 1½ HOURS ·

Carrot cake is a recipe I found surprisingly hard to veganize. Traditionally it contains quite a few eggs, which give it structure and support the rising process. Fortunately, after a lot of testing I figured out a combination of ingredients — vegan egg replacer, baking powder and apple cider vinegar — that help it rise and give it an amazing texture.

Carrot Cake

2 tbsp (30 mL) powdered egg replacer

¼ cup (60 mL) water

2 cups (500 mL) all-purpose flour

2 tsp (10 mL) baking soda

2 tsp (10 mL) baking powder

1 tsp (5 mL) salt

¼ tsp (1 mL) ground nutmeg

1 tbsp (15 mL) ground cinnamon

2 cups (500 mL) organic cane sugar

¾ cup (175 mL) vegetable oil

¾ cup (175 mL) unsweetened applesauce

1 tbsp (15 mL) apple cider vinegar

3 cups (750 mL) grated carrots

Cream Cheese Frosting

6 oz (175 g) vegan cream cheese, softened

⅓ cup (75 mL) vegan butter

1 tsp (5 mL) vanilla extract

1 tsp (5 mL) freshly squeezed lemon juice

3 to 4 cups (750 mL to 1 L) confectioners' (icing) sugar

13- by 9-inch (33 by 23 cm) metal baking pan, greased and floured

Electric mixer

1. **CARROT CAKE:** Preheat the oven to 350°F (180°C).

2. Whisk together the egg replacer and water in a small bowl. Set aside.

3. Whisk together the flour, baking soda, baking powder, salt, nutmeg and cinnamon in a large bowl.

CONTINUED ON PAGE 188

4. Place the sugar, oil, applesauce, apple cider vinegar and egg replacer mixture in a separate large bowl; stir to combine. Add the applesauce mixture to the flour mixture and stir until just combined. Add the grated carrots and stir to combine.

5. Pour into the prepared pan and smooth out the top. Bake for 1 hour or until a toothpick inserted in the center comes out with a few crumbs attached. Remove the cake from the oven and let cool completely in the pan on a wire rack.

6. **CREAM CHEESE FROSTING:** Meanwhile, cream together the vegan cream cheese and vegan butter in a large bowl, using the electric mixer. Add the vanilla extract and lemon juice; beat for about 1 minute, until smooth.

7. Gradually add the confectioners' sugar, ½ cup (125 mL) at a time, beating between additions, until combined, light and fluffy. You may not need all the sugar — the frosting should be stiff enough that it does not drip off the beaters when lifted from the bowl.

8. Frost the top of the cake, using a knife; serve. (If you would like to frost the sides, invert the cake onto a serving platter, then spread frosting over the sides and top.)

My Tip

Once frosted, this cake can be stored in an airtight container in the fridge for up to 4 days.

Fast and Fluffy No-Rise Cinnamon Rolls

• SERVES 8 • • TIME: 40 MINUTES •

I've always loved the idea of baking cinnamon rolls — their delicious warm, sweet smell makes any day feel like Christmas morning. However, I used to shy away from making them myself because I didn't like waiting around for the dough to rise. This recipe doesn't require any yeast or rising time and takes only 40 minutes from start to finish, as opposed to a few hours.

2 cups (500 mL) all-purpose flour (approx.)

4 tsp (20 mL) baking powder

3 tbsp (45 mL) organic cane sugar

¼ cup (60 mL) cold vegan butter

⅔ cup (150 mL) unsweetened nondairy milk (approx.)

3 tbsp (45 mL) softened vegan butter

⅓ cup (75 mL) lightly packed brown sugar

2 tsp (10 mL) ground cinnamon

Pastry blender (optional)

Rimmed baking sheet, lined with parchment paper

1. Preheat the oven to 400°F (200°C).

2. Whisk together the flour, baking powder and cane sugar in a large bowl. Cut in the cold vegan butter with a pastry blender or two knives, until the mixture becomes crumbly and resembles sand. Pour in the nondairy milk and stir until it just forms a dough. If the dough is a bit dry, add 1 tsp (5 mL) more milk at a time until it forms a dough but is not too sticky.

3. Remove the dough from the bowl and turn it out onto a lightly floured surface. Knead the dough 8 times, then roll it out into a long rectangle about 12 inches (30 cm) long and 6 inches (15 cm) wide. Arrange it with one long side facing you.

4. Spread the softened vegan butter over the dough, leaving a 1-inch (2.5 cm) border along the long edge that is farthest from you.

CONTINUED ON PAGE 190

5. Whisk together the brown sugar and cinnamon in a small bowl. Spread it over the buttered dough in an even layer, avoiding the 1-inch (2.5 cm) dry strip.

6. Begin rolling up the dough like a jelly roll, tugging it up and over the filling to keep it tight. Pinch the edge lightly to seal, then slice the roll into 8 pieces. Space the cinnamon rolls 2 inches (5 cm) apart on the prepared baking sheet.

7. Bake in the preheated oven for 12 to 14 minutes, until firm to the touch and golden brown. Remove from the oven and let cool on the pan for 5 minutes. Remove the rolls from the pan and serve immediately or let cool completely and store in an airtight container in the fridge for up to 3 days.

My Tip

For an extra-decadent twist, I serve these with Cream Cheese Frosting (recipe on page 187) spread on top. I prefer to halve the recipe so I don't have too much left over.

My Tips

If you can't find soft vegan margarine, you can substitute vegan butter or coconut oil plus an additional 2 tbsp (30 mL) unsweetened nondairy milk.

If you are using a very dark metal pan, bake the cookies for 9 to 10 minutes. If you're using a light metal pan, bake for 11 to 12 minutes.

Chewy Chocolate Chip Cookies

• MAKES 15 COOKIES • ⭘ 🍴 • TIME: 30 MINUTES •

These cookies are loved by everyone who tries them (ask YouTube — it's one of my most popular recipes). I always make a double batch when I have friends coming over, because no one can resist warm, chewy chocolate chip cookies. These are always gone in seconds.

1½ cups (375 mL) all-purpose flour

1 tsp (5 mL) baking soda

1 tsp (5 mL) baking powder

¼ tsp (1 mL) salt

½ cup (125 mL) soft vegan margarine (see My Tips)

1 cup (250 mL) lightly packed brown sugar

¼ cup (60 mL) unsweetened nondairy milk

1 tsp (5 mL) vanilla extract

⅓ cup (75 mL) vegan chocolate chips

Sea salt (optional)

Baking sheet, lined with parchment paper

1. Preheat the oven to 350°F (180°C).

2. Whisk together the flour, baking soda, baking powder and salt in a medium bowl.

3. Cream together the vegan margarine and brown sugar in a large bowl. Add the nondairy milk and vanilla; stir to combine.

4. Add half the flour mixture to the brown sugar mixture; stir to combine. Add the other half of the flour mixture and the chocolate chips; stir until a dough forms.

5. Spoon 1½ tbsp (22 mL) dough for each cookie onto the prepared baking sheet, spacing them 2 inches (5 cm) apart.

6. Bake in the preheated oven for 9 to 12 minutes (see My Tips), until starting to turn golden brown on top. Remove from the oven and let cool on the baking sheet for 5 minutes, then transfer to a wire rack to cool for at least 5 more minutes. Sprinkle with sea salt (if using). Serve warm or let cool completely and store in an airtight container at room temperature for up to 5 days.

Chocolate Walnut Cookie Bars

• MAKES 12 COOKIE BARS • ⬚ 🍴 • TIME: 30 MINUTES •

Cookie bars are one of my go-to desserts to take to parties and family dinners. They're basically a giant cookie baked in a pan and sliced into squares. Bonus: they're easy to transport — just take them in the same pan you baked them in. If you are not a nut person, feel free to leave out the walnuts. I like their crunch and the boost of healthy omega-3's they add, but the bars are still delicious without them.

1½ cups (375 mL) all-purpose flour

1 tsp (5 mL) baking soda

1 tsp (5 mL) baking powder

¼ tsp (1 mL) salt

¼ cup (60 mL) unsweetened cocoa powder

½ cup (125 mL) softened vegan butter

1 cup (250 mL) lightly packed brown sugar

¼ cup (60 mL) unsweetened nondairy milk

1 tsp (5 mL) vanilla extract

¼ cup (60 mL) vegan chocolate chips

¼ cup (60 mL) chopped walnuts

8-inch (20 cm) square metal baking pan

1. Preheat the oven to 350°F (180°C).

2. Whisk together the flour, baking soda, baking powder, salt and cocoa powder in a medium bowl.

3. Cream together the vegan butter and brown sugar in a large bowl, until light and fluffy. Add the nondairy milk and vanilla; stir to combine.

4. Add half of the flour mixture to the brown sugar mixture and stir to combine. Add the remaining flour mixture, chocolate chips and walnuts. Stir to form a dough.

5. Press evenly into the pan. Bake in the preheated oven for 20 minutes, until the top is slightly puffed. Remove from the oven and let cool in the pan for 5 for 10 minutes before slicing into 12 bars. Serve warm or cool (see My Tip).

My Tip
The cooled cookie bars can be stored in an airtight container at room temperature for up to 4 days or in the fridge for up to 1 week.

No-Bake Brownie Bites

• MAKES ABOUT 24 BITES • • TIME: 10 MINUTES •

I love these brownie bites because they can be made in about 10 minutes and there's no baking required. I make them when I am craving something chocolatey but with a healthy twist. The dates provide a natural sweetness and make these bites extra gooey. If you want to make a batch but don't think you'll eat them all up in a few days, you can store them in the freezer in an airtight container for up to 1 month.

1½ cups (375 mL) walnuts or pecans

2 cups (500 mL) Medjool dates, pitted

½ cup (125 mL) unsweetened cocoa powder

1 tsp (5 mL) vanilla extract

¼ tsp (1 mL) salt

Food processor

1. Combine the walnuts, dates, cocoa powder, vanilla and salt in a food processor. Process for about 3 minutes, stopping the motor periodically to scrape the sides of the bowl, until a dough forms. For each bite, scoop 1 tbsp (15 mL) dough into your hands and roll it into a ball; place on a baking sheet in a single layer. Repeat until no mixture remains.

2. Refrigerate for 1 hour, until firm. Serve or transfer to an airtight container and store in the fridge for up to 4 days or freeze for up to 1 month.

My Tip

Take this recipe a step further by lightly rolling each ball in unsweetened cocoa powder. It's a great way to make these brownie bites look a bit fancier for a dinner party or as a gift for a friend.

Deep Dish Apple Pie with Caramel Sauce

• SERVES 6 TO 8 • • TIME: 1 HOUR 30 MINUTES •

My grandmother used to make this recipe for my dad when he was a kid. His favorite way to eat it was with a scoop of vanilla ice cream and her homemade caramel sauce. I was so happy to discover that it's actually very easy to recreate vegan-style — and don't forget the vegan vanilla ice cream!

Crust

2 cups (500 mL) unbleached all-purpose flour (approx.)

2 tbsp (30 mL) organic cane sugar

¾ cup (175 mL) cold vegetable shortening

3 tbsp (45 mL) cold water

Filling

½ cup (125 mL) organic cane sugar

2 tsp (10 mL) ground cinnamon

½ tsp (2 mL) ground nutmeg

8 cups (2 L) peeled, sliced baking apples (about 6 large apples; see My Tip, page 199)

2 tbsp (30 mL) water

1 recipe Caramel Sauce (page 27) or store-bought, warmed

Vegan vanilla ice cream (optional)

Pastry blender (optional)

9-inch (23 cm) ovenproof bowl, about 4 inches (10 cm) deep, or 10-cup (2.5 L) casserole dish

1. **CRUST:** Combine the flour and sugar in a large bowl. Using a pastry blender or two knives, cut in the vegetable shortening until the mixture is crumbly and resembles sand. Add the cold water and stir to form a dough. Form the dough into a disk and wrap completely with plastic wrap. Refrigerate for at least 30 minutes or up to 1 day. (If you leave it in the fridge for longer than 30 minutes, let it warm up to room temperature before rolling.)

2. Preheat the oven to 375°F (190°C).

3. **FILLING:** Meanwhile, whisk together the sugar, cinnamon and nutmeg in a small bowl. Set aside.

CONTINUED ON PAGE 199

4. Place the apples in the ovenproof bowl and sprinkle with the sugar mixture; stir to combine. Drizzle the water overtop.

5. Sprinkle some all-purpose flour on a piece of parchment paper or wax paper. Roll out the pastry into a circle about 10 inches (25 cm) in diameter (or to fit the dish) and ¼ inch (0.5 cm) thick. Using the paper, flip the pastry over the bowl; peel off the paper. Use a knife to trim off any excess pastry hanging over the edge of the bowl. Tuck the edges of the pastry inside the rim of the bowl. Pierce the pastry with a fork or knife in several places to allow steam to escape.

6. Bake in the preheated oven for 40 minutes, until golden brown. Remove from the oven and let cool slightly before serving in bowls. Drizzle with caramel sauce and serve with a scoop of vegan vanilla ice cream (if using).

My Tip

Cortland, Granny Smith and Ida Red apples are some of the best varieties to use for baking, because they hold their shape when cooked.

Edible Cookie Dough

• MAKES 1¼ CUPS (300 ML) • ◯ • TIME: 10 MINUTES •

Like many kids, my favorite part of making cookies was sneaking some dough while my mom wasn't looking. Although, thinking back, I'm sure she also sneaked in a taste of cookie dough while I wasn't looking! This version is safe to eat raw, since it doesn't contain eggs or wheat flour. Serve by itself or on top of pancakes, ice cream or graham crackers.

1¾ cups (425 mL) oat flour (see My Tip)

¼ tsp (1 mL) salt

¼ cup (60 mL) softened vegan butter

½ cup (125 mL) lightly packed brown sugar

2 tbsp (30 mL) unsweetened nondairy milk

½ tsp (2 mL) vanilla extract

¼ cup (60 mL) vegan chocolate chips

1. Whisk together the oat flour and salt in a medium bowl.

2. Cream together the vegan butter and brown sugar in a separate medium bowl, until smooth and combined. Add the nondairy milk and vanilla; stir to combine.

3. Add the flour mixture to the brown sugar mixture; stir until a dough forms. Stir in the chocolate chips. Serve immediately or store in an airtight container in the fridge for up to 1 week or the freezer for up to 1 month.

My Tip

If you can't find oat flour, don't worry! You can easily make your own by processing 1¾ cups (425 mL) large-flake (old-fashioned) or quick-cooking rolled oats in a blender or food processor until it has a fine, flour-like consistency. Use a fine-mesh sieve to sift the result, as any pieces of oat hull will need to be removed to achieve a smooth cookie dough consistency.

My Tips

Store the cooled gingerbread cake in an airtight container, separate from the caramel sauce, at room temperature for up to 2 days or in the fridge up to 4 days. When ready to serve, reheat individual pieces in the microwave on Medium until warm. To reheat the caramel sauce, place in a microwave-safe bowl and microwave, pausing to stir occasionally, until hot. The sauce will appear very thick before heating but, once hot, it will thin out. Drizzle the sauce over the cake just before serving.

Gingerbread Cake with Caramel Sauce

• SERVES 9 • • TIME: 1 HOUR 15 MINUTES •

The spices in this cake instantly remind me of curling up with a good book and a cup of tea on a crisp fall afternoon. While gingerbread in cookie form is a traditional holiday treat, I always opt for this moist, fluffy gingerbread cake instead. It has all the spices and flavor you expect from gingerbread, and it's irresistible with a drizzle of caramel sauce and a dollop of coconut whipped cream.

2 cups (500 mL) all-purpose flour

1 tsp (5 mL) baking soda

½ tsp (2 mL) baking powder

¼ tsp (1 mL) salt

1 tsp (5 mL) ground ginger

1 tsp (5 mL) ground cinnamon

1 tsp (5 mL) ground allspice

⅓ cup (75 mL) vegetable shortening

½ cup (125 mL) organic cane sugar

1 cup (250 mL) light (fancy) molasses

¼ cup (60 mL) unsweetened applesauce

1 cup (250 mL) hot orange pekoe tea

1 recipe Caramel Sauce (page 27), warmed

Coconut whipped cream (optional)

8-inch (20 cm) square metal baking pan, greased

1. Preheat the oven to 350°F (180°C).

2. Whisk together the flour, baking soda, baking powder, salt, ginger, cinnamon and allspice in a medium bowl.

3. Cream together the shortening and sugar in a large bowl, until well combined. Add the molasses and applesauce; stir to combine. Add the hot tea; stir to combine. Add the flour mixture; stir to combine.

4. Pour the batter into the prepared baking pan. Bake in the preheated oven for 40 to 45 minutes, or until a toothpick inserted in the center comes out with a few crumbs attached.

5. Remove from the oven and let cool in the pan on a wire rack for 10 minutes before slicing. Serve warm, with caramel sauce drizzled over each slice and a dollop of coconut whipped cream (if using).

Chocolate Raspberry Mini Cakes

• SERVES 4 • • TIME: 30 MINUTES •

As a tried-and-tested sweet-lover, I enjoy any excuse to make personal-size desserts so that I don't have to share! This recipe is perfect for when you're having friends over, because it's super easy and looks impressive with its dusting of confectioners' sugar and some fresh raspberries on top. Not only are these cakes really pretty, the raspberries taste amazing with the chocolate.

1 cup (250 mL) all-purpose flour

¾ cup (175 mL) organic cane sugar

¼ cup (60 mL) unsweetened cocoa powder

1 tsp (5 mL) baking powder

1 cup (250 mL) unsweetened nondairy milk

¼ cup (60 mL) vegetable oil

⅓ cup (60 mL) vegan chocolate chips

¼ cup (60 mL) confectioners' (icing) sugar

½ cup (125 mL) fresh raspberries

4 6-oz (175 mL) ramekins

1. Preheat the oven to 350°F (180°C).

2. Whisk together the flour, sugar, cocoa powder and baking powder in a medium bowl. Add the nondairy milk, oil and chocolate chips; stir to combine.

3. Divide the batter evenly among the 4 ramekins. Bake in the preheated oven for 22 to 26 minutes, or until a toothpick inserted in the center comes out with a few crumbs attached.

4. Remove from the oven and let cool for 10 minutes. Sprinkle each cake with confectioners' sugar and top with a few raspberries. Serve warm.

My Tip
The cooled cakes can be stored in an airtight container at room temperature for up to 2 days.

My Tip
Where I live, peaches are in season for only a short time each year. If you're using canned sliced peaches, simply drain and rinse them in a mesh strainer, then measure out 2 cups (500 mL) and proceed with the recipe as directed.

Rosalie's Peach Cobbler

• SERVES 4 TO 6   ⓥ   TIME: 1 HOUR •

This recipe was passed down to me from my grandmother Rosalie. The cobbler was very easy to veganize, requiring only substitution of almond milk and vegan butter for the dairy versions. This recipe can easily be adapted depending on the time of year: use fresh peaches when they are in season and canned when fresh aren't an option.

¾ cup + 2 tbsp (205 mL) unbleached all-purpose flour

2 tbsp (30 mL) organic cane sugar

2 tsp (10 mL) baking powder

½ tsp (2 mL) salt

2 tbsp (30 mL) cold vegan shortening

⅓ cup (75 mL) unsweetened nondairy milk

2 cups (500 mL) sliced fresh or drained canned peaches (see My Tip)

½ cup (125 mL) lightly packed brown sugar

1 tbsp (15 mL) freshly squeezed lemon juice

¼ tsp (1 mL) ground cinnamon

⅛ tsp (0.5 mL) ground nutmeg

2 tbsp (30 mL) vegan butter

Coconut whipped cream (optional)

Vegan vanilla ice cream (optional)

6-cup (1.5 L) casserole dish

Pastry blender (optional)

1. Preheat the oven to 350°F (180°C).

2. Whisk together the flour, cane sugar, baking powder and salt in a large bowl. Using a pastry blender or two knives, cut in the shortening until the mixture becomes crumbly. Pour in the nondairy milk and stir to combine.

3. Combine the peaches, brown sugar, lemon juice, cinnamon and nutmeg in a medium bowl; stir to coat. Transfer to the casserole dish. Scatter pea-size pieces of the vegan butter evenly overtop.

4. Use a small spoon to drop clumps of batter over the peaches until they are completely covered.

5. Bake in the preheated oven for 40 minutes, until the top is golden brown and a tester inserted in the center comes out clean. Remove from the oven and let stand for 10 minutes before serving. Serve warm, with coconut whipped cream or vegan vanilla ice cream (if using).

Strawberry Shortcakes

• SERVES 8 • • TIME: 30 MINUTES •

Don't let the appearance of these shortcakes discourage you — I promise you, this recipe is a total cinch to make! All you need are ripe fresh strawberries and some pantry staples. The biscuit recipe is almost identical to my Breakfast Tea Biscuits (page 56), but since this is dessert, they are a bit sweeter.

Crushed Strawberries

1½ lbs (750 g) fresh strawberries, stems removed

3 tbsp (45 mL) organic cane sugar

Sweet Biscuits

1½ cups (375 mL) unbleached all-purpose flour (approx.)

1 tbsp (15 mL) organic cane sugar

2 tsp (10 mL) baking powder

¼ tsp (1 mL) salt

½ cup (125 mL) unsweetened nondairy milk

2 tsp (10 mL) white vinegar

3 tbsp (45 mL) cold vegan butter

Coconut whipped cream (optional)

Pastry blender (optional)

2.5-inch (5 cm) thin-edged drinking glass or biscuit cutter

1. **CRUSHED STRAWBERRIES:** Place the strawberries in a large bowl. Using a potato masher or fork, lightly mash the berries until juice is released and they are slightly broken up. Add the sugar and stir to combine. Refrigerate until ready to use.

2. **SWEET BISCUITS:** Preheat the oven to 425°F (220°C).

3. Whisk together the flour, sugar, baking powder and salt in a large bowl.

4. Combine the nondairy milk and vinegar in a measuring cup or medium bowl. Set aside for 5 minutes.

CONTINUED ON PAGE 210

5. Meanwhile, using a pastry blender or two knives, cut the vegan butter into the flour mixture until it becomes crumbly. Add 6 tablespoons (90 mL) of the milk mixture and stir until a dough forms (you want the dough to be slightly sticky but not too wet). Depending on the temperature and humidity at the time of baking, you may need more of the milk mixture (discard any that remains).

6. Gently knead the dough in the bowl 3 or 4 times, until it just gathers into a ball. Transfer to a lightly floured work surface and pat the dough into a disk approximately ½ inch (1 cm) thick. Using the drinking glass or biscuit cutter dipped in flour, cut the dough into large rounds, twisting the cutter slightly when it gets to the bottom. Reroll the scraps of dough as needed to make 8 biscuits.

7. Place the biscuits on a baking sheet in two rows, right next to each other. Bake in the preheated oven for 10 minutes, until the biscuits puff up and begin to turn golden brown on the bottom. Remove from the oven and let cool on the sheet for 2 minutes.

8. Slice the biscuits in half. Using a ladle, spoon crushed strawberries over each bottom half, followed by a dollop of coconut whipped cream (if using). Top with the other half of the biscuit. Serve.

My Tip

If you want to serve these at a party, you can make the biscuits a day ahead, let them cool completely and store them in an airtight container at room temperature. The crushed berries can be made a day ahead and stored in a separate airtight container in the fridge. When ready to serve, the biscuits can be individually warmed slightly in the microwave. Then proceed with Step 8 to serve.

Chocolate Zucchini Cupcakes with Mocha Frosting

• MAKES 12 CUPCAKES • • TIME: 45 MINUTES •

These cupcakes have a slightly denser consistency than most cupcakes, but they taste decadent enough to be a dessert. The zucchini adds some extra nutrition but is barely detectable in these moist, deliciously chocolatey treats. The coffee-infused mocha frosting complements the chocolate perfectly.

Cupcakes

1¾ cups (425 mL) all-purpose flour

¼ cup (60 mL) unsweetened cocoa powder

2 tsp (10 mL) baking powder

1 tsp (5 mL) baking soda

⅔ cup (150 mL) organic cane sugar

⅔ cup (150 mL) unsweetened nondairy milk

⅓ cup (75 mL) vegetable oil

2 tbsp (30 mL) white vinegar

1 tsp (5 mL) vanilla extract

1 cup (250 mL) lightly packed shredded zucchini

Mocha Frosting

3 tbsp (45 mL) vegan butter, melted

3 tbsp (45 mL) unsweetened cocoa powder

2 tbsp (30 mL) unsweetened nondairy milk (approx.)

½ tsp (2 mL) vanilla extract

3 cups (750 mL) confectioners' (icing) sugar, divided

½ tsp (2 mL) instant coffee granules

12-cup muffin tin, lined with paper liners

Electric mixer (optional)

1. **CUPCAKES:** Preheat the oven to 350°F (180°C).

2. Whisk together the flour, cocoa powder, baking powder, baking soda and sugar in a large bowl.

3. Stir together the nondairy milk, oil, vinegar, vanilla and zucchini in a medium bowl.

4. Add the zucchini mixture to the flour mixture and stir until just combined.

CONTINUED ON PAGE 213

5. Spoon the batter into the prepared muffin tin, filling the cups about 3/4 full. Bake in the preheated oven for 18 to 20 minutes, or until a toothpick inserted in the center comes out with a few crumbs attached. Remove the cupcakes from the oven and let cool for 5 minutes in the tin, then transfer them to a wire rack to cool completely before frosting.

6. **MOCHA FROSTING:** Place the melted vegan butter, cocoa powder, nondairy milk and vanilla in a large bowl; stir to combine.

7. Using an electric mixer, beat in ½ cup (125 mL) of the confectioners' sugar and all of the instant coffee; beat for about 1 minute, until smooth. Add the remaining confectioners' sugar ½ cup (125 mL) at a time; beat for about 2 minutes, until smooth. (You can also do this by hand, but incorporate just ¼ cup/60 mL of the sugar at a time.) Add 1 tsp (5 mL) more milk if the mixture is too dry. Frost the cupcakes, using a knife; serve.

My Tip

The frosted cupcakes can be stored in an airtight container in the fridge for up to 4 days.

Vanilla Birthday Cupcakes

• MAKES 12 CUPCAKES • • TIME: 35 MINUTES •

I'm pretty sure the universal rule is that everything is more fun with sprinkles, and these vanilla cupcakes are no exception. They are perfect for birthdays and other celebratory events. The cupcakes contain applesauce, which cuts down on the amount of oil you have to use. But don't worry — they are still super moist and fluffy!

Cupcakes

1½ cups (375 mL) all-purpose flour

1 cup (250 mL) organic cane sugar

1½ tsp (7 mL) baking powder

½ tsp (2 mL) baking soda

1 cup (250 mL) unsweetened nondairy milk

1 tsp (5 mL) white vinegar

¼ cup (60 mL) vegetable oil

¼ cup (60 mL) unsweetened applesauce

1 tsp (5 mL) vanilla extract

¼ cup (60 mL) sprinkles (approx.)

Buttercream Frosting

¾ cup (175 mL) vegan butter, softened

1 tsp (5 mL) vanilla extract

2½ cups (625 mL) confectioners' (icing) sugar

2 tbsp (30 mL) unsweetened nondairy milk

12-cup muffin tin, lined with paper liners

Electric mixer

1. **CUPCAKES:** Preheat the oven to 350°F (180°C).

2. Whisk together the flour, sugar, baking powder and baking soda in a large bowl.

3. Combine the nondairy milk, vinegar, oil, applesauce and vanilla in a medium bowl. Add the applesauce mixture to the flour mixture and stir until just combined (do not overmix; a few lumps are okay). Add the sprinkles and, using a spatula, fold gently 2 or 3 times to incorporate.

CONTINUED ON PAGE 216

4. Spoon into the prepared muffin tin, filling the cups about ¾ full. Bake in the preheated oven for 20 to 22 minutes, until slightly firm to the touch and a toothpick inserted in the center comes out with a few crumbs attached. Remove from the oven and let the cupcakes cool in the tin on a wire rack for 5 minutes, then remove them from the pan and transfer to a wire rack to cool completely.

5. **BUTTERCREAM FROSTING:** Meanwhile, place the vegan butter and vanilla in a large bowl. Using an electric mixer, beat until combined. Add the confectioners' sugar ½ cup (125 mL) at a time, beating until fully incorporated. Beat in the nondairy milk 1 tbsp (15 mL) at a time, as needed, to create a thick, smooth consistency.

6. Spread the frosting on the cupcakes with a knife and decorate with more sprinkles on top. Serve.

My Tip

The frosted cupcakes can be stored in an airtight container in the fridge for up to 4 days.

Marble Freezer Fudge

This freezer fudge is a no-fuss, no-bake dessert. It literally melts in your mouth, thanks to the combination of coconut oil and nut butter. Finding vegan fudge at a bakery can be nearly impossible, which is why I love making my own at home.

1½ cups (375 mL) smooth cashew butter or almond butter

6 tbsp (90 mL) coconut oil

¼ cup (60 mL) pure maple syrup or agave nectar

½ tsp (2 mL) salt

2 tbsp (30 mL) unsweetened cocoa powder

8-inch (20 cm) square baking pan, lined with parchment paper

1. Whisk together the cashew butter, coconut oil, maple syrup and salt in a large bowl. Pour half the mixture into a medium bowl and add the cocoa powder; stir to combine.

2. Alternate pouring about ¼ of each mixture into the pan, then use a knife to swirl the two flavors to give a marble effect. Place in the freezer for 4 hours. Use the parchment paper to remove the fudge from the pan and place it on a cutting board to slice. Serve immediately or transfer the pieces of fudge to an airtight container and store in the freezer for up to 1 month.

Acknowledgments

It is a dream come true to write a book and be able to share my favorite vegan recipes with you all. However, I never would have had the opportunity to do it without the help of a ton of amazing people.

First, to everyone who has ever watched my videos, tried a recipe or connected with me online, thank you. Without your support this could never have been possible. Your kind words and excitement about vegan food are the reason I do this, and they remind me every day how lucky I am to be a part of such an incredible community.

A huge thank-you to the Robert Rose team: Robert Dees, Meredith Dees, Kelly Glover, and Martine Quibell for believing in me and making this book possible. I am forever grateful for all the time and effort you all gave to this book to make sure it was the best it could possibly be. A big thank-you also to Jennifer MacKenzie and Gillian Watts for their technical and copy edits.

Thank you to the incredibly talented and creative photographer, Brilynn Ferguson, stylists Dara Sutin and Rayna Schwartz, and designer Margaux Keres for bringing the recipes to life in such a beautiful way.

To Mom and Dad: I wouldn't be who I am today without you. I love you so much! Thank you to Bridget for always making me laugh until my cheeks hurt, and for being the best sister anyone could ask for.

Thank you to my amazing friends Hannah, Emma and Kathryn. You are as excited as I am about vegan food and are always willing to try my creations. Thanks for constantly being up for brunch whenever I need a break.

Thank you, everyone, from the bottom of my heart for making this book possible. I couldn't have done it without you!

Index

A

almonds. *See also* almond butter
Almond Parmesan, 140
Almond Ricotta, 20
Broccoli Quinoa Salad
with Creamy Cashew
Dressing, 143
Vanilla Almond Butter, 26
Vegan Snackboard with Easy
Spreadable Cheese, 82
almond butter
Almond Butter Toast with
Caramelized Bananas, 49
Cashew Milk Two Ways, 10
Maple Curry Penne, 169
Marble Freezer Fudge, 217
Orange Almond Butter
Sauce, 14
Overnight Muesli, 40
Thai Peanut Sauce, 16
Warm Apples and Almond
Butter Bowls, 48
apples and applesauce
Carrot Cake with Cream
Cheese Frosting, 187
Deep Dish Apple Pie with
Caramel Sauce, 197
Simple Apple and Kale
Salad, 144
Warm Apples and Almond
Butter Bowls, 48
avocados
Avocado Fried Toast, 70
Cheesy Warm Nachos, 74
Crispy Avocado Open-Face
Sandwiches, 59
Five-Minute Guacamole, 78
Spicy "Sausage" Tacos, 155
Sweet Chili Tofu and Rice
Bowls, 174
Sweet Sriracha Cauliflower
Wraps, 131

B

bananas
Almond Butter Toast with
Caramelized Bananas, 49
Berry Smoothie Bowls, 36
Chocolate Chip Banana Bread
in a Mug, 89
Chocolate-Dipped Fruit
Pops, 86
Empty-Jar Overnight
Oats (tip), 43
Half-Baked Cookie Dough
Pancakes, 52
My Favorite Banana Bread, 184
Overnight Muesli, 40
Post-Workout Choco
Smoothie, 32
Pre-Workout Berry
Smoothie, 32
Strawberry Citrus
Smoothie, 31
Tropical Green Smoothie, 35
barbecue sauce
BBQ Tofu–Stuffed Pita
Pockets, 133
Buffalo Chickpea Wraps, 128
Hawaiian-ish Pizza, 163
Saucy Seitan Sandwiches, 152
Basil, Tomato and Parmesan
Pasta Salad, 140
Basil Cream, 118
BBQ Tofu–Stuffed Pita
Pockets, 133
beans
Black Bean and Corn
Tacos, 159
Cheesy Warm Nachos, 74
Sesame Mixed Vegetables, 106
berries. *See also specific berries*
Berry Smoothie Bowls, 36
Chocolate Raspberry Mini
Cakes, 204

Overnight Muesli, 40
Post-Workout Choco
Smoothie, 32
Pre-Workout Berry
Smoothie, 32
Vegan Snackboard with Easy
Spreadable Cheese, 82
Best-Ever Tofu Cubes, 22
biscuits, 56, 208
Black Bean and Corn Tacos, 159
blueberries
Berry Smoothie Bowls, 36
Blueberry Pie Oatmeal, 44
Empty-Jar Overnight
Oats (tip), 43
Post-Workout Choco
Smoothie, 32
bread (as ingredient). *See also*
sandwiches and wraps
Almond Butter Toast with
Caramelized Bananas, 49
Avocado Fried Toast, 70
Caesar Salad with Garlicky
Croutons, 148
Cheesy Toasted Garlic
Bread, 117
Southwest Scramble Toast, 63
Breakfast Tea Biscuits, 56
broccoli
Broccoli Quinoa Salad
with Creamy Cashew
Dressing, 143
Broccoli with Cheese
Sauce, 113
Sesame Mixed Vegetables, 106
Takeout Thai Curry Coconut
Soup, 97
brunch menu, 6
Buffalo Chickpea Wraps, 128

C

cabbage
  Dragon Noodles, 181
  Thai Spiral Noodle Salad, 139
Caesar Salad with Garlicky
    Croutons, 148
Cajun-Spiced Wedges, 121
Caprese Pizza, 164
Caramel Sauce, 27
  Deep Dish Apple Pie with
    Caramel Sauce, 197
  Gingerbread Cake with Caramel
    Sauce, 203
carrots. See also vegetables
  BBQ Tofu–Stuffed Pita
    Pockets, 133
  Broccoli Quinoa Salad with
    Creamy Cashew
    Dressing, 143
  Carrot Cake with Cream Cheese
    Frosting, 187
  Cheese Sauce, 19
  Chickpea Tuna Pita Pockets, 134
  Ginger-Glazed Carrots, 110
  Lentil Chili, 160
  Spaghetti Squash Pad Thai, 177
  Takeout Thai Curry Coconut
    Soup, 97
  Thai Spiral Noodle Salad, 139
cashews. See also cashew butter
  soaking, 4
  Basil Cream, 118
  Cashew Milk Two Ways, 10
  Cheese Sauce, 19
  Crispy Avocado Open-Face
    Sandwiches, 59
  Easy Spreadable Cheese, 82
  Red Pepper Fettuccini, 170
cashew butter
  Creamy Cashew Dressing, 143
  Marble Freezer Fudge, 217
cauliflower
  Cheesy Vegetable Soup, 98
  Sesame Mixed Vegetables, 106
  Sweet Sriracha Cauliflower
    Wraps, 131
  Sweet Sriracha Roasted
    Cauliflower, 109

cereals, 39–47
cheese (vegan). See also Cheese
    Sauce; specific types (below)
  Caprese Pizza, 164
  Cheesy Toasted Garlic
    Bread, 117
  Chickpea Tuna Pita Pockets, 134
  Cream Cheese Frosting, 187
  Gooey Grilled Cheese
    Sandwiches, 130
  Hawaiian-ish Pizza, 163
  Spicy "Sausage" Tacos, 155
  Sun-Dried Tomato and Spinach
    Pinwheels, 85
cheese, Parmesan (vegan), 140
  Basil, Tomato and Parmesan
    Pasta Salad, 140
  Lemon Asparagus Risotto, 173
  Simple Apple and Kale
    Salad, 144
  Untraditional "Chicken"
    Parmesan, 156
cheese, ricotta (vegan), 20
  Caprese Pizza, 164
  Famous Lasagna Soup, 94
  Gooey Grilled Cheese
    Sandwiches, 130
Cheese Sauce, 19
  Broccoli with Cheese Sauce, 113
  Cheesy Warm Nachos, 74
  Mac and Cheese Bake, 166
Cheesy Vegetable Soup, 98
Chewy Chocolate Chip
    Cookies, 193
chia seeds
  Chocolate Chia Pudding, 81
  Empty-Jar Overnight Oats, 43
  Overnight Muesli, 40
  Pre-Workout Berry
    Smoothie, 32
  Tropical Green Smoothie, 35
"Chicken" Parmesan,
    Untraditional, 156
chickpeas
  Buffalo Chickpea Wraps, 128
  Chickpea, Lentil and Sweet
    Potato Curry, 165
  Chickpea Scramble, 61

Chickpea Tuna Pita Pockets, 134
chocolate. See also cocoa powder
  Chewy Chocolate Chip
    Cookies, 193
  Chocolate Chip Banana Bread in
    a Mug, 89
  Chocolate-Dipped
    Fruit Pops, 86
  Chocolate Raspberry Mini
    Cakes, 204
  Chocolate Walnut
    Cookie Bars, 194
  Edible Cookie Dough, 200
  Empty-Jar Overnight
    Oats (tip), 43
  Vegan Snackboard with Easy
    Spreadable Cheese, 82
Cinnamon Peach Oatmeal, 47
Cinnamon Rolls, Fast and Fluffy
    No-Rise, 189
cocoa powder. See also chocolate
  Chocolate Chia Pudding, 81
  Chocolate Zucchini Cupcakes
    with Mocha Frosting, 211
  Marble Freezer Fudge, 217
  Mini Chocolate Lava
    Pancakes, 51
  No-Bake Brownie Bites, 196
  Sweet and Salty
    Popcorn (tip), 73
Coconut Granola, Spiced, 39
coconut milk
  Chickpea, Lentil and Sweet
    Potato Curry, 165
  Cream of Mushroom Soup, 104
  Maple Curry Penne, 169
  Roasted Butternut Squash
    Soup, 102
  Takeout Thai Curry Coconut
    Soup, 97
  Thai Coconut Rice, 107
corn
  Black Bean and Corn Tacos, 159
  East Coast–Style Chowder, 101
  Vegetable Fried Rice, 178
cranberries (dried)
  Simple Apple and Kale
    Salad, 144

Sweet Potato Salad with Spiced Maple Dressing, 136
Cream of Mushroom Soup, 104
Creamy Hummus Salad Dressing, 15
Crispy Avocado Open-Face Sandwiches, 59
Crispy Baked Onion Rings, 124
Crispy Breakfast Potatoes, 55
Crispy Tofu Dippers, 69
cucumber
  Basil, Tomato and Parmesan Pasta Salad, 140
  Summery Quinoa Salad, 147
  Sweet Chili Tofu and Rice Bowls, 174
  Vegan Snackboard with Easy Spreadable Cheese, 82
cupcakes, 211–16

D
Deep Dish Apple Pie with Caramel Sauce, 197
dinner party menu, 6
dips and sauces, 12–19, 78
Dragon Noodles, 181

E
East Coast–Style Chowder, 101
Edible Cookie Dough, 200
Empty-Jar Overnight Oats, 43

F
Famous Lasagna Soup, 94
Fast and Fluffy No-Rise Cinnamon Rolls, 189
Five-Minute Guacamole, 78
flax seeds (ground)
  Post-Workout Choco Smoothie, 32
  Strawberry Citrus Smoothie, 31
Fruit Pops, Chocolate-Dipped, 86
fruit (dried)
  No-Bake Brownie Bites, 196
  Overnight Muesli, 40
  Simple Apple and Kale Salad, 144

Sweet Potato Salad with Spiced Maple Dressing, 136
Vegan Snackboard with Easy Spreadable Cheese, 82

G
Gingerbread Cake with Caramel Sauce, 203
Ginger-Glazed Carrots, 110
gluten, vital wheat. See seitan
Gooey Grilled Cheese Sandwiches, 130
Gravy, Veggie, 13
greens. See also lettuce; spinach
  BBQ Tofu–Stuffed Pita Pockets, 133
  Crispy Avocado Open-Face Sandwiches, 59
  Simple Apple and Kale Salad, 144
Guacamole, Five-Minute, 78

H
Half-Baked Cookie Dough Pancakes, 52
Hawaiian-ish Pizza, 163
holiday dinner menu, 6
"Honey Mustard" Dip, Vegan, 17
Hummus Salad Dressing, Creamy, 15

K
kitchen supplies, 2–3

L
Lemon Asparagus Risotto, 173
lentils
  Chickpea, Lentil and Sweet Potato Curry, 165
  Famous Lasagna Soup, 94
  Lentil Chili, 160
  Summery Quinoa Salad, 147
lettuce. See also greens
  Buffalo Chickpea Wraps, 128
  Caesar Salad with Garlicky Croutons, 148
  Chickpea Tuna Pita Pockets, 134
  Spicy "Sausage" Tacos, 155
  Sweet Sriracha Cauliflower Wraps, 131

lime juice
  Spicy Lime Mayo, 18
  Spicy Mango Salsa, 78

M
Mac and Cheese Bake, 166
mangos
  Spicy Mango Salsa, 78
  Tropical Green Smoothie, 35
maple syrup
  Chocolate Chia Pudding, 81
  Maple Cinnamon Pecans, 77
  Maple Curry Penne, 169
  Roasted Butternut Squash Soup, 102
  Spiced Maple Dressing, 136
  Sweet and Salty Popcorn, 73
Marble Freezer Fudge, 217
Marinara Sauce, 12
mayonnaise (vegan)
  Buttermilk-Style Dressing, 135
  Curry Mayo, 123
  Ranch Sauce, 131
  Spicy Lime Mayo, 18
  Vegan "Honey Mustard" Dip, 17
menus, 6–7
milk (nondairy). See also coconut milk
  Chocolate Chia Pudding, 81
  Cinnamon Peach Oatmeal, 47
  Crispy Baked Onion Rings, 124
  East Coast–Style Chowder, 101
  Empty-Jar Overnight Oats, 43
  Half-Baked Cookie Dough Pancakes, 52
  Mini Chocolate Lava Pancakes, 51
  Overnight Muesli, 40
  Post-Workout Choco Smoothie, 32
molasses
  Caramel Sauce, 27
  Gingerbread Cake with Caramel Sauce, 203
mug cakes, 89–90
mushrooms
  Cream of Mushroom Soup, 104
  Famous Lasagna Soup, 94
  Savory Breakfast Bowls, 64
My Favorite Banana Bread, 184

N

Nachos, Cheesy Warm, 74
No-Bake Brownie Bites, 196
noodles. *See also* pasta
    Dragon Noodles, 181
    Takeout Thai Curry Coconut
      Soup, 97
    Thai Spiral Noodle Salad, 139

O

oats and oat flour
    Blueberry Pie Oatmeal, 44
    Cinnamon Peach Oatmeal, 47
    Edible Cookie Dough, 200
    Empty-Jar Overnight Oats, 43
    Overnight Muesli, 40
    Spiced Coconut Granola, 39
Onion Rings, Crispy Baked, 124
orange juice
    Berry Smoothie Bowls, 36
    Orange Almond Butter
      Sauce, 14
    Pre-Workout Berry
      Smoothie, 32
    Strawberry Citrus Smoothie, 31
outdoor summer meal menu, 7
Overnight Muesli, 40

P

pancakes, 51–52
pasta. *See also* noodles
    Basil, Tomato and Parmesan
      Pasta Salad, 140
    Famous Lasagna Soup, 94
    Mac and Cheese Bake, 166
    Maple Curry Penne, 169
    Red Pepper Fettuccini, 170
    Untraditional "Chicken"
      Parmesan, 156
peaches
    Cinnamon Peach Oatmeal, 47
    Rosalie's Peach Cobbler, 207
    Tropical Green Smoothie, 35

peanut butter
    Overnight Muesli, 40
    Spaghetti Squash Pad Thai, 177
    Thai Peanut Sauce, 16
    Thai Spiral Noodle Salad, 139
pecans
    Maple Cinnamon Pecans, 77
    No-Bake Brownie Bites, 196
    Spiced Coconut Granola, 39
    Strawberry Spinach Salad
      with Buttermilk-Style
      Dressing, 135
    Sweet Potato Salad with Spiced
      Maple Dressing, 136
peppers, bell. *See also* peppers,
    jalapeño; vegetables
    Black Bean and Corn Tacos, 159
    Chickpea, Lentil and Sweet
      Potato Curry, 165
    Dragon Noodles, 181
    East Coast–Style Chowder, 101
    Famous Lasagna Soup, 94
    Hawaiian-ish Pizza, 163
    Lentil Chili, 160
    Maple Curry Penne, 169
    Red Pepper Fettuccini, 170
    Southwest Scramble Toast, 63
    Spaghetti Squash Pad Thai, 177
    Summery Quinoa Salad, 147
    Takeout Thai Curry Coconut
      Soup, 97
peppers, jalapeño
    Cheesy Warm Nachos, 74
    Spicy Mango Salsa, 78
    Spicy "Sausage" Tacos, 155
Perfectly Photogenic Roasted
    Veggies, 114
pineapple
    Hawaiian-ish Pizza, 163
    Tropical Green Smoothie, 35
pitas
    BBQ Tofu–Stuffed Pita
      Pockets, 133
    Chickpea Tuna Pita Pockets, 134
pizzas, 163–64
Popcorn, Sweet and Salty, 73

Post-Workout Choco Smoothie, 32
potatoes
    Cajun-Spiced Wedges, 121
    Cheese Sauce, 19
    Cheesy Vegetable Soup, 98
    Crispy Breakfast Potatoes, 55
    East Coast–Style Chowder, 101
    Perfectly Photogenic Roasted
      Veggies, 114
    Roasted Mini Potatoes with
      Basil Cream, 118
    Super-Fluffy Mashed
      Potatoes, 120
Pre-Workout Berry
    Smoothie, 32

Q

quinoa
    Broccoli Quinoa Salad
      with Creamy Cashew
      Dressing, 143
    Savory Breakfast Bowls, 64
    Summery Quinoa Salad, 147

R

Red Pepper Fettuccini, 170
rice
    Lemon Asparagus Risotto, 173
    Sweet Chili Tofu and Rice
      Bowls, 174
    Thai Coconut Rice, 107
    Vegetable Fried Rice, 178
    Ricotta Two Ways, Vegan, 20
Roasted Butternut Squash
    Soup, 102
Roasted Mini Potatoes with Basil
    Cream, 118
Rosalie's Peach Cobbler, 207

S

salads, 135–48
salsa. *See* tomato sauces
sandwiches and wraps, 59,
    128–34, 152
sauces and dips, 12–19, 78
Savory Breakfast Bowls, 64

seitan
    Hawaiian-ish Pizza, 163
    Saucy Seitan Sandwiches, 152
    Seitan "Sausage" Crumbles, 24
    Sliceable Seitan, 25
    Spicy "Sausage" Tacos, 155
sesame oil
    Sesame Mixed Vegetables, 106
    Vegetable Fried Rice, 178
sesame seeds. *See also* tahini
    Sesame Mixed Vegetables, 106
    Thai Spiral Noodle Salad, 139
Simple Apple and Kale Salad, 144
Sliceable Seitan, 25
smoothies, 31–35
Snackboard with Easy Spreadable
    Cheese, Vegan, 82
Snickerdoodle Mug Cake, 90
soups, 94–105
Southwest Scramble Toast, 63
Spaghetti Squash Pad Thai, 177
Spiced Coconut Granola, 39
Spicy Lime Mayo, 18
Spicy Mango Salsa, 78
Spicy "Sausage" Tacos, 155
spinach. *See also* greens
    Basil, Tomato and Parmesan
        Pasta Salad, 140
    Caprese Pizza, 164
    Famous Lasagna Soup, 94
    Gooey Grilled Cheese
        Sandwiches, 130
    Maple Curry Penne, 169
    Strawberry Spinach Salad
        with Buttermilk-Style
        Dressing, 135
    Sun-Dried Tomato and Spinach
        Pinwheels, 85
    Sweet Potato Salad with Spiced
        Maple Dressing, 136
    Tropical Green Smoothie, 35
squash. *See also* zucchini
    Roasted Butternut Squash
        Soup, 102
    Spaghetti Squash Pad Thai, 177

strawberries
    Berry Smoothie Bowls, 36
    Chocolate-Dipped Fruit
        Pops, 86
    Post-Workout Choco
        Smoothie, 32
    Strawberry Citrus Smoothie, 31
    Strawberry Shortcakes, 208
    Strawberry Spinach Salad
        with Buttermilk-Style
        Dressing, 135
summer meal menu, 7
Summery Quinoa Salad, 147
Sun-Dried Tomato and Spinach
    Pinwheels, 85
Super-Fluffy Mashed
    Potatoes, 120
Sweet and Salty Popcorn, 73
Sweet Chili Tofu and Rice
    Bowls, 174
sweet potatoes
    Baked Sweet Potato Fries with
        Curry Mayo, 123
    Chickpea, Lentil and Sweet
        Potato Curry, 165
    Perfectly Photogenic Roasted
        Veggies, 114
    Savory Breakfast Bowls, 64
    Sweet Potato Salad with Spiced
        Maple Dressing, 136
sweets, 86–90, 184–217
Sweet Sriracha Cauliflower
    Wraps, 131
Sweet Sriracha Roasted
    Cauliflower, 109

T
tahini
    Creamy Cashew Dressing, 143
    Savory Breakfast Bowls, 64
    Sliceable Seitan, 25
Takeout Thai Curry Coconut
    Soup, 97
Thai Coconut Rice, 107
Thai Peanut Sauce, 16
Thai Spiral Noodle Salad, 139

toast recipes. *See* bread
tofu
    pressing, 4
    BBQ Tofu–Stuffed Pita
        Pockets, 133
    Best-Ever Tofu Cubes, 22
    Crispy Tofu Dippers, 69
    Dragon Noodles, 181
    Southwest Scramble Toast, 63
    Spaghetti Squash Pad Thai, 177
    Sweet Chili Tofu and
        Rice Bowls, 174
    Tofu Ricotta, 21
    Vegetable Fried Rice, 178
tomatoes. *See also* tomato
    sauces; vegetables
    Basil, Tomato and Parmesan
        Pasta Salad, 140
    Buffalo Chickpea Wraps, 128
    Caprese Pizza, 164
    Chickpea, Lentil and Sweet
        Potato Curry, 165
    Crispy Avocado Open-Face
        Sandwiches, 59
    Gooey Grilled Cheese
        Sandwiches, 130
    Lentil Chili, 160
    Marinara Sauce, 12
    Savory Breakfast Bowls, 64
    Spicy Mango Salsa, 78
    Sun-Dried Tomato and Spinach
        Pinwheels, 85
    Sweet Sriracha Cauliflower
        Wraps, 131
tomato sauces
    Black Bean and Corn Tacos, 159
    Caprese Pizza, 164
    Cheesy Warm Nachos, 74
    Famous Lasagna Soup, 94
    Hawaiian-ish Pizza, 163
    Spicy "Sausage" Tacos, 155
    Untraditional "Chicken"
        Parmesan, 156

tortillas
  Black Bean and Corn Tacos, 159
  Buffalo Chickpea Wraps, 128
  Southwest Scramble
    Toast (tip), 63
  Spicy "Sausage" Tacos, 155
  Sweet Sriracha Cauliflower
    Wraps, 131
Tropical Green Smoothie, 35

U

Untraditional "Chicken"
  Parmesan, 156

V

Vanilla Almond Butter, 26
Vanilla Birthday Cupcakes, 214
vegan cooking
  on a budget, 1–2
  pantry staples, 3, 10–13
  sample menus, 6–7
Vegan "Honey Mustard" Dip, 17
Vegan Ricotta Two Ways, 20
Vegan Snackboard with Easy
  Spreadable Cheese, 82
vegetables. See also greens;
    specific vegetables
  Cheesy Vegetable Soup, 98
  Lemon Asparagus Risotto, 173
  Perfectly Photogenic Roasted
    Veggies, 114
  Sesame Mixed Vegetables, 106
  Vegan Snackboard with Easy
    Spreadable Cheese, 82
  Vegetable Fried Rice, 178
Veggie Gravy, 13
vital wheat gluten. See seitan

W

walnuts
  Chocolate Walnut Cookie
    Bars, 194
  No-Bake Brownie Bites, 196
  Simple Apple and Kale
    Salad, 144
  Vegan Snackboard with Easy
    Spreadable Cheese, 82

Warm Apples and Almond Butter
  Bowls, 48
weekend dinner party menu, 6
wheat gluten, vital. See seitan

Z

zucchini
  Chocolate Zucchini Cupcakes
    with Mocha Frosting, 211
  Lentil Chili, 160
  Thai Spiral Noodle Salad, 139